Word Problems

Grades 4-5

By
Harold Torrance

Cover Illustration by
Jeff Van Kanegan

Published by

Frank Schaffer Publications®

Author: Harold Torrance
Cover Illustration: Jeff Van Kanegan
Inside Illustrations: Milton Hall
Photo Credits: © Image Club Graphics/Studio Gear

Frank Schaffer Publications®

Send all inquiries to:
Frank Schaffer Publications
8720 Orion Place
Columbus, OH 43240

Word Problems—grades 4-5

ISBN 0-7424-0135-9

5 6 7 8 9 MAZ 11 10 09 08 07 06

Introduction

Word problems have long been a source of confusion for students. Figuring out ways to teach students how to solve them has been a source of frustration for teachers as well. A student typically looks at a page of word problems with very little enthusiasm. Often a mix of fear and anger is associated with word problem activities. To make matters worse, these attitudes may have been present before students were even assigned to your class. These perceptions *can* affect the student's capacity to deal with word problems, perhaps even more than the lack of necessary computational skills.

The problems in this book are very long by the usual standards. They are written in the style of lengthy "story" problems on purpose. They describe situations encountered by people in business settings, in their homes, while working with hobbies, and in a multitude of other realistic settings. These settings will demonstrate to students the practical nature of word problems. The length also will force the student to slow down and actually *read* each problem.

Information is presented to the student in a narrative format. Sometimes the numbers needed for working a problem are revealed near the very beginning, sometimes near the end. Often other figures are thrown in, not for the sake of confusion, but to give the student the opportunity to discriminate useful information from irrelevant information.

The problems are designed to force a *new* pattern of behavior on the student. Students seem to have the notion that the words in a word problem are simply obstacles to their quickly gleaning the numbers out of the problem and doing a computation. For working word problems, speed is *not* what students need. These problems will slow them down a bit, forcing students to read and understand the problem before taking action to solve it. Once students know what the problem is about and understand what it is asking, they have probably cleared the biggest hurdle! By the time this book is finished, students ideally will have developed a new pattern of behavior for approaching word problems.

Table of Contents

Cash Register Sings at Music Store

The Music Store sells musical instruments, accessories for instruments, sheet music, instructional books, and compact discs. Music lessons also may be arranged through the store. The owner of the Music Store also possesses the skills to repair fine instruments, charging a per-hour fee for this service. These services and product offerings make the Music Store quite a successful business. The owner has even been thinking of moving the store to a better retail location. He thinks a newer storefront in a busier area would give the store even more exposure. He is considering a location where the monthly rent would be $2,350. That represents an increase of $590 beyond the store's current monthly rent. What is the owner of the Music Store currently paying for the store's monthly rent? _____

A special violin has been added to the inventory at the Music Store. The owner traveled to an auction in a distant city to purchase this instrument. He considers it to be the best item ever offered for sale in his shop. The violin is a Greater Hanoverius, a scarce and highly regarded instrument. It has already attracted a great deal of interest from his regular customers, and there also have been several inquiries about the violin from out of state. After carefully considering the price he paid and the violin's potential, the owner set a price of $16,000 for the Greater Hanoverius. In contrast, the Music Store sells an entry-level student violin for only $160. How many more times the price of the entry-level violin is the Greater Hanoverius? _____

Zoo Gets New Look

The Barton Zoo has a reputation for creative, animal-friendly exhibits. For this reason the zoo is a popular destination for both individuals and school groups. Barton Zoo houses over 1,500 animals, each living in its own specially designed exhibit. The zoo's exterior fence serves as a backup safety feature, designed as a last line of enclosure if an animal should escape from its own self-contained exhibit.

The exterior fence is old and has been repaired in a number of spots. It soon must be replaced with a better design. Companies who specialize in this type of fence work were asked to bid on the job. The best price presented to the zoo was $205,000. If the Barton Zoo's director has already arranged for $127,500 to be budgeted for the fence, how much more money must be arranged through fund-raising or from other zoo budgets for the project to proceed? _____

A generous donor with an interest in the conservation of rare bears gave the Barton Zoo $50,000. The gift comes with the condition that the money be spent either to improve existing bear exhibits or for acquiring additional animals. Barton Zoo's director has decided to buy two new bears at a cost of $14,350 each. The new bears will be housed in an existing exhibit. Another $9,600 will be spent enlarging and improving the present bear exhibits. How much of the original donation remains after these improvements are made? _____

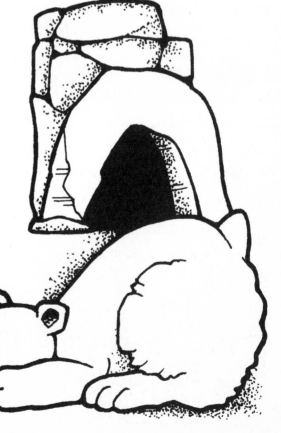

More About Barton Zoo

Too many people feed the animals at Barton Zoo. One child was recently caught feeding a hot dog (with mustard) to a porpoise. An anteater was also made sick from eating a chocolate cookie. Barton Zoo has decided that people must be made aware of the dangerous health risks involved in feeding the animals such junk foods. The zoo is having new signs made for all exhibits reminding people not to feed anything to the animals. Cost for making the 155 new signs will be $17 each. Materials and labor needed to install the signs will cost another $5 per sign. How much will the new signs cost the zoo once they are all installed? _____

Barton Zoo's insurance company has determined that volunteers may no longer work at the zoo for both safety and liability concerns. A volunteer worker recently was blamed after an expensive parrot escaped from its exhibit. The parrot flew away after a door was mistakenly left open. In insurance terminology this was a "covered event" and the insurer became responsible. A substantial expense was incurred before the parrot was finally returned to the zoo. It was after this incident that the insurance company banned volunteer workers at the zoo, threatening to cancel the insurance policy if the zoo did not comply with the rule immediately.

The insurance company still must pay the expenses involved in what has been called "that dreadful parrot episode" by several of its office staff. When it was first discovered

that the parrot was missing, a reward of $1,500 was posted immediately for the parrot's return. The parrot later turned up in the flower garden of a private residence. The insurance company paid the reward to a neighbor who saw the parrot and contacted the zoo. They also paid the owner of the garden $2,825 for damage done by the parrot to their rare orchid collection. While the parrot was being captured, it became angry and bit an employee of the zoo. The bitten employee incurred an emergency room bill of $289.60 while having the wound treated. The insurance company was responsible for all the expenses involved in recovering the parrot, even the employee's emergency room visit. How much did the parrot's escape cost the insurer? _____

Denture Business Looks Good

Ned is a salesman for a denture supply company in the Midwest. When dealing with the dentists on his customer list, Ned prefers to use the term "replacement teeth." He thinks "dentures" is a somewhat old-fashioned term which has a certain amount of negative imagery attached to it.

Ned is a big believer in the product he sells, since all of his own teeth were lost in his teens due to extremely poor dental hygiene habits and drinking too many soft drinks. Ned wears model #2230 for his uppers and the slightly more daring model #2215 for his lowers. He has caught women staring at his replacement teeth a number of times during conversations, so Ned is certain that he has chosen the right models. Ned got his teeth at a special discount under the employee benefits plan. The #2230 cost him $439.85 instead of the regular price of $499. The #2215, possibly Ned's best feature, cost him only $199.59 since the line was being gradually phased out. How much did Ned spend for his replacement teeth? _____

Ned put in a very busy week of sales calls. He travels frequently, visiting customers in their offices to make sales presentations. On Monday Ned traveled 135 miles, making 5 sales calls. On Tuesday he traveled 116 miles, getting in 8 sales calls. Wednesday was a bit slow compared to the other days, with 60 miles traveled and only 2 sales calls made. Thursday Ned visited 4 customers and traveled 37 miles. Friday was a big day, 9 sales calls and 190 miles traveled. How many miles did Ned travel this week meeting with customers? _____

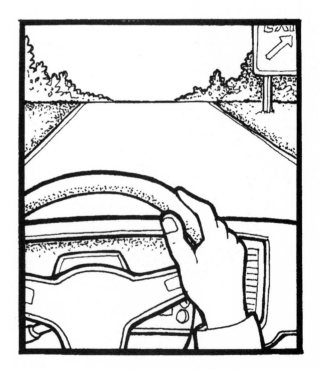

More About Ned the Denture Salesman

Ned has noticed the new trend in contact lenses, offering colors to the customer as a means of increasing sales. Ned thinks the technique would work with his company's line of replacement teeth as well. His reasoning is "Why should people be limited to just varying shades of white for their teeth color?" Ned is so confident of his new idea that he has taken several of his sales samples and dyed them different colors–nothing too overbearing, just light shades of blue, green, red, and purple. A fifth denture turned out looking almost tie-dyed after dye colors were mixed. Ned especially liked that one.

The sales manager at Ned's company was not nearly as enthusiastic when he saw the dyed denture samples, especially the one that looked tie-dyed. He told Ned that his sales commissions were going to be withheld until the company was fully reimbursed for the ruined denture samples. The manager valued the samples at $50 each. How much will this cost Ned in commissions? _____

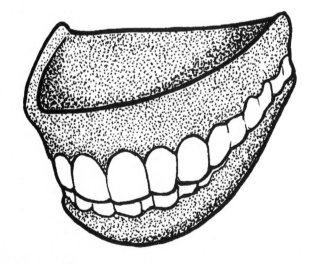

Ned recently experienced a setback with a new customer. This particular dentist told Ned that his recent denture order looked "fakey" and patients wanted refunds. After thinking about the returned order, Ned figures that his company's innovative, high quality replacement teeth products just are not for everybody. The dentist had ordered a #2212 at a cost of $455.99, a #2202 at a cost of $390.12, and a #1909 at a cost of $318. Ned will arrange a full refund for the dissatisfied dentist. How much money should the refund check be made out for? _____

A Transporting Hobby

Sean's hobby is classic cars. It seems that all his spare time is spent in pursuit of this hobby. He frequently attends automobile rallies and other car-related events. He also reads a great deal about car restoration.

Sean is in the process of restoring a classic car. He has been keeping a log of all his expenses, since he maintains a strict budget during these projects. Sean always provides the labor for these projects, so materials are his biggest expense. So far he has purchased the following items for this project: an inside door panel $61.50, a muffler $92.29, touch-up paint $17.59, a new tire $64.99, hood ornament $38.50, and engine parts $139. How much has Sean spent on this project so far? _____

Sean is considering replacing a worn-out seat in the car he is restoring. The seat is on the driver's side. This makes it a little more difficult to find a replacement, since the driver's seat is typically the one that needs replacing first. One company has a seat available for $98 plus $28 for shipping. Another company has the same model seat for $89 plus $39 for shipping. Both seats are in about the same condition. Other than price there is no advantage to ordering from one company over the other. How much will Sean save by ordering the seat from the company with the best overall deal? _____

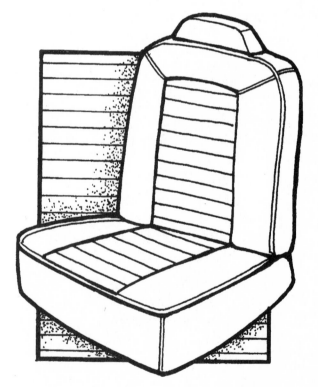

College Budget Computed

Kelly is preparing for college. She is planning to attend a nearby junior college, so expenses are not as high as they might have been otherwise. Part of her tuition will be taken care of by a scholarship. Kelly is now trying to figure how much available cash she currently has on hand. Her money is in several different savings accounts. One of the accounts was opened by her grandparents and now contains $3,145.14. The account where she keeps money from her summer jobs now has a balance of $4,818.10. An old savings account from her newspaper delivery days has $390.66 in it. Her parents also have an account designated for her college expenses with $6,550.75 in it. How much money does Kelly have available for college? _____

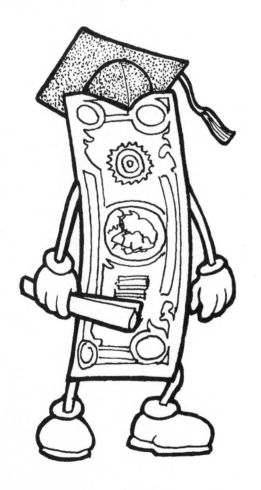

Kelly has changed her mind about attending the junior college. After thinking about this junior college and its course offerings, Kelly decided it really was not the right place for her. She is now planning to attend a rather expensive out-of-state university. The school has a special program in theater arts, a good feature since the junior college she had previously planned to attend did not even have a theater, much less a theater program. Kelly now thinks that theater will be the main focus of her studies. Tuition at the new school will run $17,730 per year for the four-year degree program. What is the cost of attending this school for four years? _____

Rainy Valley Farm Tries New Approach

Rainy Valley Farm has 260 acres under cultivation. While smaller than many commercial growers, Rainy Valley Farm is attentive to the needs of its customers. The farm's success comes from recognizing demand and trying to meet that demand with quality produce. Rainy Valley Farm currently specializes in growing table vegetables for fine restaurants. Most of its land is used for this purpose.

The balance of Rainy Valley Farm's acreage is set aside for growing seasonal items, such as pumpkins, ornamental corn, and gourds. This season Rainy Valley Farm has 24 acres planted in ornamental corn, 16 acres planted in gourds, and 41 acres planted in pumpkins. The remaining land is reserved for growing table vegetables for their restaurant clients. How many acres are planted in table vegetables? _____

The owners of Rainy Valley Farm are looking ahead to the future. They must be successful at predicting agricultural trends in order to remain competitive. Setting aside 20 acres for fruit trees is an idea currently being considered. The owners anticipate a good market for fruit in the years to come, but there is a drawback. The trees would need four years to mature before producing a saleable crop. No income would be produced by the trees during that time. The 20 acres being considered would ordinarily produce an income of $4,475 per year. If Rainy Valley Farm goes ahead with this idea, how much will they lose in income while waiting for the trees to mature? _____

More About Rainy Valley Farm

A drought at Rainy Valley Farm has led to a number of problems. The owners have to rethink their plan in regard to several fields. Crop yields will certainly be affected if adequate rains do not come soon. The decision has been made to harvest the onions early. While the onions are only half their normal size, they can still be sold. The land occupied by the onions will be replanted with a shorter crop such as lettuce, which may have a better chance of producing when the rains resume. Since the onions are only half their normal size, they will bring only half their normal amount when sold. Yearly income from the onions is usually $8,250. What will the drought-affected onions be worth? _____

Rainy Valley Farm owns several tractors. Each tractor is a different size, used for different kinds of work. They are all expensive to operate and maintain. Each has its own schedule for oil changes and other preventative maintenance. Lately, a rash of repairs has sapped the farm's maintenance budget. Now the smallest tractor at Rainy Valley Farm has an oil leak. Unfortunately, the problem went unnoticed and the tractor's engine seized up while it was being used. A repairman was called out to look at the tractor and determined that repairs would amount to $1,280. The farm's maintenance budget only contains $895. How much money will be needed from another source to pay for repairs to the tractor? _____

Modeler Meticulous About Math

Conrad has an interest in fine scale models. He collects models, maintaining them unopened in their original wrappings. Conrad also builds models. He is a stickler for detail and usually spends several months on a single project. The model he is currently building is a scale replica, in wood, of an 1800s sailing schooner.

Conrad keeps a log to let him know how many hours have been devoted to each project. According to his project log, Conrad has already spent 62 hours on the schooner. With experience, Conrad has gotten quite adept at estimating how long a particular project will take to complete. He anticipates that the schooner project will reach a conclusion at the 90-hour mark. If his estimate is correct, how many more hours of work are needed for the schooner project to be completed? _____

Conrad finds the quality of models ordinarily available in local shops to be a bit below the level of sophistication and workmanship he prefers. Conrad often orders models from faraway places to be delivered directly to his house. He is expecting a fine ship model to arrive from England any day now. Conrad prepaid $168 for this model, plus an additional charge of $42 to cover expected shipping and import duties. He has also ordered a stand for this model at a cost of $30.75 which includes delivery. Conrad also purchased paint and other related supplies in preparation for this project. Cost for those items was $28.80 at a local hobby shop. How much money has Conrad already put into this project? _____

More About Conrad and His Models

Conrad is planning to travel to an event sponsored by the New England Model, Crafters, and Doll Association. He wants to display one of his ship models in a competition there. The entry fee is only $5. First prize for winning the category is $20, plus the enormous prestige that comes with winning such a widely acclaimed award!

Conrad is preparing a budget to see what such a trip will cost. Before the competition, he would need to renew his membership with NEMCDA at a cost of $17. Travel and eating expenses will amount to $35 since he will get a friend to drive him there, paying for gasoline and their lunch. Conrad would also have to pay his regular sitter $10 to look after his dog while he is gone for the day. (His dog tends to get into mischief without supervision.) How much will it cost Conrad to attend the event and enter his model in the competition? _____

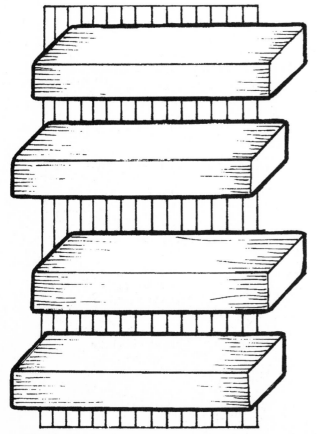

Conrad has spent $120 to buy an 8-foot section of basswood. This is a variety of wood commonly used for carving, due to its favorable characteristics. Conrad will cut the 8-foot length into 4 equal pieces, keeping 2 of those pieces for his own work and letting 2 friends each have a piece for their hobby projects. The friends have agreed to reimburse Conrad for his cost in the basswood pieces they are to receive. How much money will each friend owe Conrad? _____

Writer Keeps Up with Charges

Celeste is a freelance writer. She works on writing projects for a number of different companies but does not work full-time for any particular one. Celeste charges the companies in one of two different methods. Sometimes she agrees to do a writing job for a fee agreed upon in advance. The rest of the time, Celeste works for wages, getting paid a certain amount per hour. Either way, Celeste must be careful not to accept work that she cannot finish on time.

Celeste is currently working on an article for a magazine. She is being paid $750 for this article. Celeste also has another project pending with this magazine. When that article is finished, it will be worth $975. How much money can Celeste expect from the magazine when these two articles are completed? _____

Celeste has worked for 32 hours completing a script for a documentary film. The script will be read by a noted actor who is also working on the documentary. The producer of this documentary has mentioned to Celeste that this may be the first of a series if this production goes well. By prior agreement Celeste will receive $25 per hour for all work she performs on this project. Now that she has finished with her work, how much money will Celeste be paid for writing the script for this documentary?

_____

Free Art Show Gets Expensive

Katy has organized a small art show for three of her artist friends. A gallery owner is allowing Katy the use of an exhibit room for her special Friday and Saturday showing. Since Katy's three artist friends are all sculptors, their work will not compete with the gallery's main focus of watercolor paintings. The gallery owner figures that the sculptures being shown might attract potential customers who do not ordinarily visit the gallery, so it seems a good arrangement for everyone involved.

Even though the gallery owner is allowing the use of the exhibit room free of charge, Katy must still contend with some expenses. She has paid for a cleaning crew to come in on Sunday morning after the show to clean the exhibit room and wax the floors. The bill for that was $65. A catering service has been hired for $239.75 to provide snacks and drinks on Friday evening. Katy has also taken out an ad in a local art newspaper for $88.25 to advertise the event. Even though Katy has already paid these expenses herself, her artist friends have insisted on splitting the bill evenly among themselves and reimbursing Katy for all her expenses. (They need to wait until after the show to do this, since they all hope to sell a few sculptures.) How much money should Katy be getting from each artist after the show? _____

The gallery owner was so impressed by Katy's handling of the sculpture show that he has offered her a job arranging special events for the gallery. The gallery owner has offered to pay her a salary of $175 for organizing an event plus $45 per day for managing the event each day it stays open. How much will Katy receive from the gallery owner for arranging and managing a 5-day event? _____

Down at the Fish Market

The Port Harbor Fish Market has a convenient warehouse location near the piers. The market buys fish and other types of seafood directly from the fishermen as their boats come in. Port Harbor Fish Market then sells these seafood products "over the counter" to the general public. These kinds of sales are called **retail sales.** They also sell larger quantities to restaurants and grocery stores at discounted prices, called **wholesale sales.** Port Harbor Fish Market sells lobster retail for $11.29 per pound. The wholesale price for the same grade of lobster is $6.99 per pound. How much more per pound does Port Harbor Fish Market make on a retail lobster sale than on a wholesale lobster sale? _____

Port Harbor Fish Market has just received a large delivery of 950 pounds of shrimp. While this delivery was being processed, another 250 pounds arrived from a different source. These deliveries were a welcome sight for Port Harbor Fish Market. It had been completely out of shrimp for several days. Customers were calling with urgent shrimp orders, and Port Harbor Fish Market had nothing available to sell them.

The scarcity of shrimp was especially a problem for five of Port Harbor Fish Market's best restaurant customers. Each had large, unfilled orders pending for shrimp. Since each restaurant has been a good customer in the past, the decision has been made to split the available shrimp equally among the five. Each restaurant will end up with less shrimp than it needs, but it will have something to work with until more shrimp comes in from the fishing fleet. How many pounds of shrimp should Port Harbor Fish Market send to each restaurant? _____

More About the Port Harbor Fish Market

The manager at Port Harbor Fish Market has been studying sales trends. It is hard to make sense of these figures, due to differences in seasonal demand, occasional shortages of products, severe weather, and a host of other factors that can affect sales. However, he has noticed that sales on the last day of a month are usually lower than sales on the first day of that same month. The manager has attributed this difference to retail customers doing more buying during the first part of the month. For example, in September the sales were only $619.45 on the last day of the month. Port Harbor Fish Market sold $4,412.76 on the first day of that same month! How much more was sold by the market on the first day of September than on the last day of September? _____

The manager at Port Harbor Fish Market has also turned his attention to crab sales. He bought 135 pounds of crab from a fisherman on Wednesday and dumped the catch into a bin already containing 28 pounds of crabs. The market sold no crabs the rest of that day. However, they sold 45 pounds of crab on Thursday and 61 pounds of crab on Friday. After the close of business on Friday, the manager checked the crab bin, and, much to his surprise, it looked nearly empty. He suspects that a large number of crabs were either stolen or sent out without a proper invoice being written for them. First he must weigh the crabs still in the bin to determine what portion may be missing. How many pounds of crabs should still be in the bin?

_____

Coin Collection Keeps Hobbyist Counting

Danny has been collecting coins for a number of years. He frequently attends coin shows and club meetings associated with his hobby. Lately Danny has been trying to properly inventory his coin collection. He realizes that this will take a great deal of time, since his collection is quite sizeable. Danny has decided to begin with the Lincoln cents and work upward.

It is a daunting task, as the pennies are stored in plastic tubes, each capable of holding a standard roll of 50 coins. Danny has 43 of these tubes which are full. Another tube lacks only 5 coins being full also. While sorting his collection Danny found another tube of pennies mistakenly placed with his nickels. It contains 23 pennies. He thinks all of his pennies are now accounted for. How many pennies does Danny have? _____

Danny's Jefferson nickels have always been stored in a cardboard box. In the past as he accumulated new coins, he just threw them into the box, thinking that he would organize the collection someday. He has now decided to move the nickels into plastic storage tubes similar to those housing his pennies. A nickel tube is designed to hold a standard roll of 40 nickels. How many tubes will Danny need to purchase if he has 2,131 nickels?

_____

More About Danny and His Collection

Danny has let his coin collecting interests expand into new areas. He has never had an interest in foreign coins, but a coin dealer he has been trading with for several years has offered to sell him a 40-pound bag of world coins. The dealer is asking $125 for the coins. Danny does not know much about foreign coins, but this offer sounds like it might be a good deal. Danny figures that the canvas bag containing the coins has got to be worth at least $5. How much per pound will Danny be paying for the coins if he values the canvas bag at $5 in his computations? _____

A member of Danny's coin club has told him about a dealer in another state with pretty good prices. Danny is reluctant to do business through the mail, especially when the money must be sent before the merchandise is shipped. He will place a small order the first time to see if the dealer is trustworthy. Danny has selected a few items and is trying to figure his total before writing the check. He has selected a buffalo nickel at $2.25, an Indian head cent for $3.55, and a book about grading coins for $7.95. The dealer charges $3.35 for shipping on orders totaling under $50. Orders over that amount are not charged for shipping as a courtesy to the customer. What is the amount of the check Danny is sending to pay for his first order? _____

Time for a Helicopter Tour

Flight-Seeing Helicopter Tours operates four helicopters as part of its tour business. It runs helicopter tours near a scenic national park and offers passengers several different routes from which to choose. Each tour covers a prearranged route and lasts a preset amount of time. Passengers may choose tours according to their own interests, based on availability.

Three of Flight-Seeing's most popular tours are the Timberbreak, the Lakeshore Run, and the Mountain Circuit. The Timberbreak is the longest tour, a route covering 320 kilometers around the perimeter of the park. The Mountain Circuit, which usually books the fastest, covers 266 kilometers along a scenic mountain range. The Lakeshore Run has a route of 280 kilometers, following a stream as it flows into several lakes of varying sizes. How many more kilometers does the longest tour route cover than the shortest? _____

Flight-Seeing Helicopter Tours has added a new route to its regular schedule. The new route is called the Lakeshore Deluxe Expanded Tour, and it includes everything seen on the Lakeshore Run Tour, plus part of what is covered by the Mountain Circuit tour. Response to this new tour has been very good, and bookings are up. This new flight is the longest tour by far, lasting 99 minutes. Passengers are warned when they book this tour not to indulge in too much coffee or soft drinks before the flight! The previous longest tour was 1 hour, 5 minutes. How many minutes longer is the new Lakeshore Deluxe Expanded Tour? _____

More About Flight-Seeing Helicopter Tours

Three of Flight-Seeing's helicopters are leased monthly at a cost of $4,200 each. The fourth helicopter is a different model than the others. It is smaller and costs only $3,450 per month to lease. Flight-Seeing has found leasing to be a more cost-effective way of operating the helicopters than owning them. Of the leased helicopters, the smallest is especially useful for doing tours when not enough seats are sold to fill one of the larger helicopters. How much per month does Flight-Seeing Helicopter Tours need to set aside to pay for all of its helicopter leases? _____

Flight-Seeing's three larger helicopters will carry seven passengers in addition to the pilot. But the larger helicopters also consume substantially more fuel. From a business standpoint, it is unprofitable to run them when fewer than four seats have been sold for a tour. The small helicopter is frequently used when bookings are not sufficient to run one of the larger helicopters. But the small helicopter has a big drawback, its reduced load limit. The small helicopter can carry a total load of only 326 kilograms. Trying to carry more weight than this poses a potential safety hazard. If the pilot weighs 78 kilograms, how much weight is left for the passenger load? _____

Baskets for the Making

Julia has a home-based business selling baskets she makes by hand. She collects materials from her own farm to make these baskets. All the baskets are made from various tree barks, strips of split wood, vines, or other natural fibers. Since Julia collects the materials on her own property, the baskets cost nothing to make except her time.

Basket sales to friends and relatives went so well that Julia found herself thinking of opening a shop. She has a good product that she is convinced people will want. After making some inquiries, she located a small storefront to rent. Julia has figured that rent and utilities at this shop will cost $500 per month. These are expenses she must pay every month just to keep her shop open. Business has been good for Julia. After the first month she has managed to sell 60 baskets. She has taken in a total of $1,200, but that is not her profit. She still must pay her shop's rent and utilities. After those expenses are paid, what profit has Julia made for her first month in the shop? _____

Julia figures that the results for her first month were pretty good, especially for a brand-new business. But a problem soon arises. Julia must wait on customers and answer the phone at her shop. These constant distractions leave little time for her to actually make the baskets! Without new baskets to sell, the shop would soon be out of inventory. Julia must now hire an employee to wait on customers and answer the phone. This will increase her monthly expenses, but at the same time it will free Julia to concentrate on making more baskets for the shop's inventory.

After running an ad in the local paper, Julia found an employee willing to work part-time in the shop. The new employee will be paid $650 per month.

Now Julia is at the end of her second month in the shop. For the second month she has sold a total of $1,420 in baskets. From this amount she must still pay rent and utilities of $500, plus her employee's salary of $650. How much profit has Julia made for her second month in the shop after the rent and salary expenses are paid? _____

Hikers Learn by Doing

Tom and Lisa recently decided to take a
hiking trip along a segment of the Appalachian Trail.
They originally got the idea from friends who have done it before.
Neither of them had ever tried an outdoor vacation before, instead preferring luxury
resorts or cruise ships. But the idea of hiking and camping seemed intriguing and the
two decided to give it a try.

Since they had no gear for such an outing, both would need a backpack, a sleeping
bag, and hiking boots. Tom selected a backpack priced at $189.95, a sleeping bag for
$79.50, and hiking boots for $225. Lisa's backpack was slightly less expensive, $179.
But her sleeping bag was much more expensive, costing $139. She found hiking boots
she liked for $199.99. The two also selected a camp stove at a cost of $90. Tom and
Lisa figured that these expenses were less than the cost of a cruise and that the gear
could be used over again, so the initial cost did not really seem too excessive. The two
will borrow the rest of the equipment they need from friends. How much money have
Tom and Lisa spent so far to get the hiking trip started?_____

Tom and Lisa returned from their trip feeling
like they needed another vacation to rest up
from the one they had just taken! Over a
period of five days, the two walked 68 miles.
They had also been soaked to the skin by
rain nearly every day and bothered by
mosquitoes almost the whole time. Tom
and Lisa have had a chance to discuss their
trip and evaluate what to do differently the
next time. One point of concern was their
pace. They covered only 9 miles the first day
and 11 miles on the second day. They then
felt rushed to get to their prearranged
meeting point where a friend would be
picking them up by car. How many miles
did they have to cover over the last 3 days of
their hike to reach the prearranged meeting
point? _____

Stocks Hold Investor's Interest

Lois has been investing in stocks for a number of years. (A share of stock represents a small piece of ownership in a company.) Lois prefers owning stocks to keeping her money in a bank account. She understands that there is financial risk involved in owning stocks, but she thinks that stocks will give her a better return on her investment monies in the years to come.

Lois did a bit of research into a copper mining company. After considering the company's potential for earning profits in the years to come, she decided to invest in this company. Lois bought 225 shares of stock in the copper mining company at $7 per share. What was her total cost for this stock purchase? _____

Profit is made when shares of stock are sold for a higher price than was initially paid. But sometimes money can be lost investing in stocks. If the price of a stock drops after you have purchased it, then money will be lost if the stock is sold at those lower levels. Lois owns 10 shares of stock in a banking company. She originally paid $119 per share for this company's stock. The price of the stock has appreciated over a period of several years. It is now worth $206 per share. If Lois were to sell her 10 shares of stock in this company, how much profit would she make on the stock? _____

More About Stocks

Lois recently had lunch with a friend who shared an interesting stock tip. Her friend mentioned a horse farm with a reputation for producing successful race horses. The farm was in the process of issuing stock to sell to potential investors. After checking into the opportunity, Lois decided to buy 100 shares of the farm's stock at $21 per share. The company's financial background looked a bit shaky, but Lois was intrigued by the idea of investing in a race horse farm. As the months passed, Lois watched the price of this stock decline. Upon reflection, she realized that it had not been a wise investment decision. When the stock reached $9 per share, Lois sold all her shares in the race horse farm. How much money did she lose on this investment? _____

Lois has experienced a number of recent setbacks with her stock investments. She was greatly alarmed to hear a news report about a shipping company that had lost its entire fleet to a hurricane. Unfortunately, the name of this shipping company was all too familiar to Lois, as she owns some of its stock. Lois originally paid $4 per share for the 175 shares she owns. She thinks her investment may be a total loss. If the company's stock becomes worthless after this disaster, how much money does Lois stand to lose? _____

Books Become Unwanted Clutter

Eric has a large number of both paperback and hardback books around his house–by his count, way too many. He bought a lot of the books himself, but many were given to him by friends and relatives. The books grew in number over the years to the point where they now take up far too much space. Eric has no interest in keeping most of these books. Some he has read, while others represent areas he has no interest in. To him, the books have become just so much clutter!

Eric began by sorting the books in his home office, setting aside 280 unwanted books. He decided to drop off these books at the thrift store. But before he could do this, Eric needed to buy boxes to pack up the books. He thinks smaller-sized boxes are best for lifting and loading the books into his van. If one box will hold 20 books, how many boxes will Eric need to buy? _____

One room at Eric's house had no furniture in it, just piles of stacked books. This small room had always been an extra room, but over time it had become so cluttered with books that it became useless for anything else. Eric decided that this room was beyond his own capability to sort, so he called used-book dealers until he found one who was interested. The book dealer brought his assistant and loaded the books into their truck in just a couple of hours. Eric decided that he would use the money he made from the sale of the books to buy a few pieces of furniture for the room, which now looked very empty. The room measures 12 feet by 10 feet. How many square feet of floor space does Eric have to work with in this room?

_____

Hockey Fan Keeps Close Count

Bradley is a big hockey fan, and he is trying to lose weight. However, Bradley finds it very difficult during hockey season to follow his regular diet. This is because Bradley drinks too many soft drinks and eats too many snacks while watching the hockey games. He gets nearly all the hockey games by subscription over his satellite dish and has plenty of opportunities to eat while watching them. Bradley's normal weight of 188 pounds tends to creep upward to 220 pounds during hockey season. This weight gain has happened several years in a row. How much weight does Bradley tend to gain during hockey season? _____

Bradley travels to a distant city's stadium several times a year to see hockey games played in person. Going to the games is both expensive and time consuming. Bradley has a number of different ways to pass the time during these trips. One way he keeps occupied is by timing his trips to the stadium and making comparisons in his travel log.

Last season Bradley drove to the stadium for three hockey games. Driving to the first game took 49 minutes. The roads were surprisingly clear for his trip to the second game, and he reached the stadium in only 37 minutes. His trip to the third game took exactly one hour due to bad weather. How many minutes separated the longest trip to the stadium from the shortest trip? _____

Kennel Dilemma

Elizabeth's family owns a dog kennel. The kennel has a good reputation as a long-time breeder of both Newfoundlands and Malamutes. The dogs are raised for both showing and working. Once purchased, their clients use the dogs in a number of settings, as companions, for hunting, and even for pulling sleds.

Some months back, one of the Newfoundlands got into a pen with one of the Malamutes. The mistake was not discovered before it was too late. An odd-looking litter of puppies was the result. Elizabeth calls these puppies New-Muts. (Neighbors who have seen the puppies agree with the name, especially the last syllable.) Due to their mixed heritage, the puppies have no commercial value and cannot be sold. But Elizabeth would still like to see them all placed in caring, responsible homes. She has purchased useful items for each of the five puppies, assembling a kit of sorts to get them off to a good start in their new homes. The kits are all identical and each contains items such as toys, leashes, canned food, and plastic dishes. Elizabeth spent a total of $175 on the kits. How much money is that per puppy? _____

The father of one of Elizabeth's friends works for a pet food distributor. He recently gave Elizabeth 80 pounds of large dog biscuits. The dog biscuits were in boxes and bags which were damaged and could not be sent out to pet stores for their inventories. Elizabeth plans to make use of this unexpected gift. She will give each of the family's 16 dogs a biscuit per day as a treat until the biscuits run out. If there are six of these large biscuits per pound, how many days will the 80-pound supply last? _____

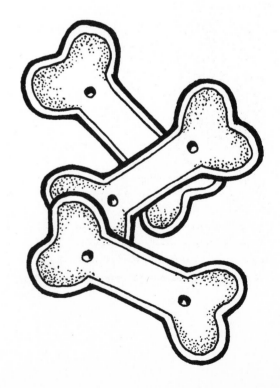

More About Elizabeth and the Kennels

Elizabeth has been making improvements to the kennels, pens, and exercise areas. This includes routine chores, such as repairing fences and reroofing the doghouses. She has also been trying to address some nonessential areas that relate to how well the dogs enjoy their surroundings. Elizabeth has installed speakers inside nine of the doghouses so the dogs can listen to the radio in the evenings. She knows that the dogs really appreciate these kinds of little luxuries. This little luxury has cost Elizabeth a total of $279 to do all the doghouses involved. Purchasing the speakers and installing them cost the same amount per doghouse. How much money was spent per doghouse for this improvement? _____

Elizabeth has selected one of the Malamutes to train as a show dog. Since she probably would now be showing the dog, she went ahead and paid the $45 fee to have it registered with an association. She then put the young dog on a training schedule, teaching it how to respond under the leash and how to stand properly for evaluation by the show judges. This young Malamute seems to hold a lot of promise, so Elizabeth paid an advance entry fee of $35 to get him into an upcoming show. She also bought a new collar and leash to use at the show at a cost of $24.89 and a special dog shampoo for $6.29. The only other show expense Elizabeth can think of will be the parking fee of $4 at the arena. By the time she gets this dog to the show, how much will Elizabeth have spent on all the fees and supplies? _____

Dairy Delivers the Goods

Ernest works for the Happy Cows Dairy Farm in upstate Oregon. The dairy still offers a delivery service to local customers who wish to have milk, cream, and cheese delivered directly to their homes. The dairy has found the practice to be cost effective and allows them access to customers who would not go to the trouble of driving to their Happy Cows Dairy Store. The dairy stays competitive by not charging any extra for their delivery service beyond the prices that would ordinarily be seen in the supermarket.

Ernest is a delivery driver for the dairy and manages the accounts of customers along his route. He works Monday through Friday driving his route. Ernest makes 90 deliveries per day. This includes placing the customer's order in a cold box on the porch and adding extra items if the customer has left a note. How many deliveries per week does Ernest make? _____

Ernest has been asked by the dairy's owners if he would like to take on a short route on Saturday mornings. They are looking for someone to take over the route but need someone in the interim until the right driver can be found. Ernest is considering it. The dairy wants him to work from 7:30 a.m. until the deliveries are finished and will pay $60 per Saturday if he will do it. Ernest thinks he can be finished with the route by 10:30 a.m., since it is much shorter than his regular daily routes. How much will Ernest make per hour if he decides to fill in for the Saturday route? _____

32

More About Happy Cows Dairy Farm

Happy Cows Dairy Farm is celebrating its seventy-fifth year in business by giving its home delivery customers a free quart of milk if their regular weekly milk order is two or more quarts. The milk will come in a special carton denoting the occasion. The anniversary milk offer is really a way of showing customers that they would probably use that extra quart of milk per week, so it is as much a marketing gimmick as an anniversary gift. The dairy's owners are hoping that many of the home delivery customers will increase their regular weekly orders after realizing that they can use the extra milk each week. The special offer will cause Ernest extra work. He has to lug 280 extra one-quart containers of milk along on his route that week. How many extra gallons of milk will he be delivering during the dairy's anniversary week as a result of the free milk promotion? _____

The Happy Cows Dairy Farm is buying four new trucks for the delivery routes. Ernest is especially looking forward to this since his old truck is one of the vehicles being replaced. All the new trucks will be custom fitted with coolers and racks, making them more expensive than base-model trucks. The largest truck will cost $38,750. It is for the heavy grocery store route. A mid-sized truck at a cost of $33,325.85 will be used for the largest of the home delivery routes. Ernest is getting one of two trucks that are identical. They are smaller in size and intended for the normal home delivery routes. They will cost $28,999.59 each. How much is the dairy spending to put all these new trucks into service? _____

Writers' Group Wears Out Welcome

Sharon has been a member of a writers' support group for several years. The group first began when a few people with a common interest in writing got together to discuss writing projects, techniques, and career opportunities. The group also provides feedback on members' written work. Meetings initially were held at members' houses on an alternating basis.

Gradually, the writing group members began dropping hints that Sharon was by far the best hostess and that the group could most comfortably meet at her house instead of alternating. Sharon was hesitant at first but agreed when the other members promised to provide the refreshments for the meetings. Word soon spread about the group, and new members began joining. Pretty soon it turned into quite a large group every week, and Sharon was stuck providing the refreshments when the other members forgot. Sharon would not have been too concerned except that the group consumes food like a pack of hungry wild animals. Last week she put out 12 dozen doughnuts at a cost of $2 per dozen and two 12-packs of soft drinks at a cost of $4 per 12-pack. The group ate every morsel! How much did Sharon spend on the group for refreshments last week? _____

Sharon still meets with the writers' group, but now they rent a meeting room at a nearby hotel convention center. Each member shares the cost of the meeting room and the catering. So many people started attending that a need quickly arose for a club treasurer to handle monies. Naturally, Sharon was "volunteered" for the post. Since there was no money in the club treasury, Sharon collected $5 in dues from each of the 23 people in attendance and also added her own dues to the club fund. She then paid the hotel $40 for the meeting room rental and another $68 for the food served to the group. After paying these expenses, how much money was left in the club treasury for the next meeting? _____

More About Sharon the Writer

Sharon has been hired to write the biography of a minor celebrity. Her publisher has promised her a big film star for the next biography if she does a good job with this one. The publisher wants 220 pages for this project, with an emphasis on the celebrity's childhood memories, early career experiences, and interesting on-set movie stories. A meeting has been arranged between Sharon and the minor celebrity, but the celebrity can spend only 40 minutes on the interview. (Sharon has already been told by her publisher that she will be "making up a lot of the material" for this book.) The publisher is paying Sharon $9,020 for writing this book. How much money is that per page? _____

Sharon recently finished a manuscript she had been working on for several months. It was not assigned work, so she now must convince a publisher to purchase the manuscript. She has selected three publishers and needs to send a copy of the manuscript to each publisher for review. It will cost Sharon $7.20 per manuscript for copies. It will also cost her $12 per manuscript for overnight delivery. How much money will Sharon spend to copy and send these manuscripts to the selected publishers? _____

Volunteer Club Puts in the Time

The Volunteer Club is an after-school club. Members donate their time around the school and occasionally assist community volunteer organizations. The club has 15 members.

The school library has just had new shelves installed. The workmen took all the books off the old shelves before installing the new ones, so a giant clutter of books has been left behind. The Volunteer Club is spending a Saturday helping the school librarian reshelve the books. Only 12 members are able to help with this particular project, each offering to work a 2-hour shift. Four of the club's members have also agreed to work an additional 2-hour shift on Sunday. How many total hours will the Volunteer Club have donated to the library reshelving effort after the weekend volunteering is done? _____

A special project will require 7 Volunteer Club members to travel to a nearby city. They have been invited by a restoration group to clean up yards and paint houses in a historic area of the city. Various organizations are involved in the project. The Volunteer Club members who are participating have agreed to work 8 hours each, except for one club member who must leave early and will be donating only 4 hours. How many hours will the club, as a whole, donate to this project? _____

Walking Club Goes the Distance

Marie and several of her neighborhood friends take regular walks together. The walks are not any sort of organized activity. Those who want to go just tag along when they see the group forming. Several people in the group began calling it "the walking club," even though nothing formal has ever been arranged.

The group ordinarily assembles at about the same time each morning at the neighborhood playground. The walkers chat for a while and wait to see who will show up for that day's walk. At some point they decide on the course for the day and then get started. Marie and 5 other people showed up for Tuesday's walk. The group went 3 miles that day. How many total miles were walked by the "walking club" on Tuesday's walk? _____

Marie was disappointed to see that only two other people showed up at the playground for Thursday's walk. It looked a bit like it might rain, so that probably kept the others away. One of the two already there was carrying an umbrella–just in case. On this day the group kept up a consistent, brisk pace. They covered 4 miles in just 56 minutes. This was a little faster than normal, probably due to the small group size and the threat of getting caught in the rain if they tarried. On average, how long did it take them to walk each mile? _____

37

Art Studies Prove Innovative

Maya is an art student. From an early age Maya seemed to show a great deal of creativity in her artistic expression. Her parents arranged a number of beneficial experiences for Maya as she was growing up. This included private lessons, summer art camps, and cooperative experiences. By the time Maya finished high school, she was already an accomplished artist. It seemed both logical and natural for her development to continue in the direction of the arts.

Maya does not study through a traditional college or university setting. Her education is now being provided under the supervision of several noted artists. Maya studies with one artist for a set time period. She then is sent to study with another artist, creating a kind of circuit. Several art students are being advanced in this manner. Each is provided with opportunities to study under all of the teaching artists involved. Maya's program has her studying with four artists over a period of one year. If an equal amount of time is to be spent studying with each artist, how many months will Maya spend with each one? _____

Maya's favorite teacher is Jacqueline. Jacqueline was once a noted sculptress but is no longer able to handle the tools due to her frail physical condition. Her strength now lies in guiding the work of others.

Maya thinks Jacqueline is about 80 years old, although she will not discuss her age, except to say she has "seen quite a lot of new inventions come into play." Maya thinks that she may have solved this riddle though. One day Jacqueline let it slip that she was 43 years old when she completed a somewhat renowned sculpture called the **Dancing Swans.** Maya looked up the sculpture in an art catalog and saw that it was listed as being completed 39 years ago. If Maya's information is correct, how old would that make Jacqueline? _____

More About Maya the Artist

Maya is finished with her studies and now producing works of her own. A gallery has agreed to represent her. The gallery owner gets one half of the sale price of any painting that sells through the gallery. Maya thinks that she will be able to negotiate a better deal once she is more established, but this arrangement is okay for now.

During the first month only one of Maya's paintings was sold, a flower study priced at $240. The second month was much better–three paintings sold. The first was a landscape that was priced at $420. The second painting was another flower study that went for $210. The sale of the third painting was a bit of a surprise. It was an experimental piece Maya created representing the street she lives on. She did not really have high expectations for it, but the gallery owner managed to sell it for $620. How much money will Maya receive for her paintings sold during the second month? _____

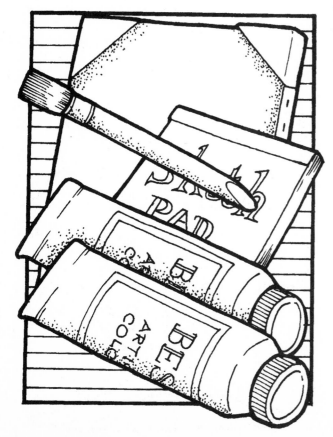

The gallery owner has arranged for Maya to have an account at a local art store. Anytime she needs materials she can charge them to her account at the art store, and the gallery owner pays for them. Maya sees this as the biggest perk in her arrangement with the gallery. In a one-week period Maya charged a canvas at a cost of $20.55, a paintbrush for $18.25, a sketchpad that cost $10.95, and two tubes of paint at $7.75 each. How much was the gallery owner responsible for paying to the art store for this particular week on Maya's behalf? _____

Who Fixes All Those Old Watches?

Mr. Goldman owns a watch repair shop. Goldman's is open from 9 a.m. until 5 p.m. weekdays only. Mr. Goldman's business is built around repairing fine pocket watches. He enjoys a reputation as something of a pocket-watch expert. In addition to his own shop customers, Mr. Goldman is frequently called on by other dealers to evaluate watches. He charges nothing to evaluate a pocket watch for repair. If he is able to fix the watch, he charges a flat fee of $10 plus $1 per minute for each minute he spends working on the watch. How much would Mr. Goldman bill a customer for a watch repair taking 12 minutes? _____

Mr. Goldman bought an antique pocket watch from one of his regular customers for $45. The customer had owned the watch for a number of years, but it had never worked. The watch was not only missing parts, but it had sustained damage from a severe shaking. The watch looked a bit hopeless to begin with, but Mr. Goldman made something of a hobby out of the project. He gradually located the difficult-to-find parts through a dealer parts network and worked on the watch in his spare time. He eventually spent a total of $138.55 on parts for the watch. After much time and effort, Mr. Goldman was able to put the watch back in working order. He placed the watch in the shop's inventory, and it eventually sold for $400. How much profit did Mr. Goldman make?

_____

More About Mr. Goldman's Shop

Mr. Goldman is considering adding a new line of business to his watch repair shop. He wants to find some new inventory item or service to offer his customers, since pocket watches no longer seem to represent a growth area. A friend has suggested that he try carrying a variety of nose rings and belly button rings. He could then perform the piercings for an added fee. Mr. Goldman did not think this idea was quite right for his shop. He has instead decided to carry a line of expensive replacement watch bands. All the watch bands will be priced so that Mr. Goldman makes a profit of $19.95 each time one is sold. As a service he will also install the replacement band on the customer's watch for an added fee of $4.75. How much money will Mr. Goldman make each time a replacement band is sold and the band is installed? _____

Goldman's has been selected by the Northeast Guild of Pocket Watch Craftsmen to host the organization's annual convention. This will not pose an inconvenience for Mr. Goldman since the guild has only 4 other members. Ordinarily, the annual convention just means playing cards in the back room of the shop belonging to that year's host. However, Mr. Goldman has decided to do something special for this year's convention. He will have the event catered by Maxine's Fine Catering. Maxine owes Mr. Goldman $140 for parts and labor on a pocket watch repair and has offered to provide the catering to settle this bill. How much per person does this catered meal cost?

_____

Teacher Tries New Strategy

Luke is a new teacher. He is somewhat envious of the other teachers who have had years to accumulate good instructional supplies for their classrooms. Luke is concerned that the materials provided by the school district where he works are not sufficient for what he thinks his classes will need.

Luke has decided to spend $200 of his own money at the beginning of the school year to buy classroom materials he thinks will be useful for teaching. The first item Luke plans to buy is a special scientific graphing calculator. The model he wants will cost $48.49. How much will be left of Luke's fund for other supplies after he pays for this calculator? _____

Luke has noticed that there are 12 different forms that must be filled out if a teacher wants to obtain supplies through the school district central office. The different forms pertain to whether items ordered are consumable supplies such as paper, nonconsumable supplies such as staplers, what department the supplies are intended for, and a variety of other circumstances. If the requesting teacher fills out an incorrect form, then the order is not filled. Luke is not very hopeful. A teacher who works with him just received a box full of supplies he had ordered through the district supply system. However, the order was placed 3 years ago.

Luke figures that he will need materials for his classroom more quickly than the district office is able to supply. He has placed an order with E-Office, "the largest supplier of school and office products on the Net." Luke has chosen 2-day shipping for his order at a cost of $23.75. Regular shipping would have cost only $14.45, but it would have taken a week for his order to arrive. How much money could Luke have saved by going with regular shipping?

_____

Data Collecting Looks Fishy

Valerie and Jackson are volunteering for an environmental group. They have been asked to collect information "in the field." Their assignment will be watching a stream and counting the salmon that pass by their viewpoint to spawn upstream. The data will then be analyzed by biologists who work with the group.

Valerie and Jackson have decided to take turns working at their assigned viewpoint. One of them will take the clipboard and count fish for half an hour, then the other person will take a turn. Their assigned shift is four hours. The two counted a total of 176 salmon during their assigned shift. On average, how many salmon passed their viewpoint per hour? _____

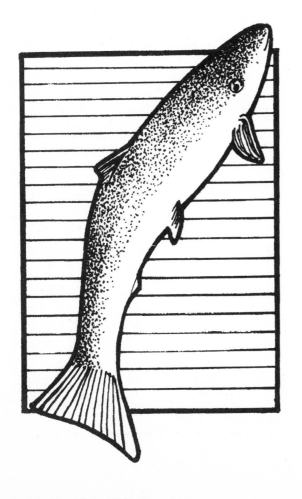

Valerie and Jackson were later told that 75 two-person volunteer teams were sent out at the same time to collect data about the salmon. All of the teams involved worked four-hour shifts at different geographic locations. The data collection project was quite important to the environmental group sponsoring it. The data would be used by biologists to estimate fish populations in each of the different locations. This information would give the environmental group an idea what course of action it needed to take for helping to conserve the fish populations studied. How many total hours were spent by the volunteers collecting the information for this salmon research project? _____

The Lure of Old-World Travel

Louise and her friend Michele have had an active interest in Italy for a number of years. The two have shared numerous books and brochures on the subject. Louise has even taken lessons in an attempt to learn a bit of the language. The two had always thought of Italy as a faraway place, which would be far too expensive to ever visit. Louise was quite surprised when Michele called her one day to tell her that plans for a trip to Italy were in the making.

Michele's travel agent located a villa in Italy that could be rented for an entire month at a cost of $2,895. The travel agent also found an airfare special for only $495 per person. After a frenzied budgeting session, Louise and Michele figured that food and other expenses could be managed for a total of $845. If the two intend to split all rent, fares, and other expenses equally, how much money will each need to set aside for the vacation? _____

Louise and Michele arrived to find the villa in excellent condition. Everything appeared just as they had hoped it would be. The two did get one small "surprise." Upon arrival the leasing agent mentioned to them that both the villa's cook and the villa's maid were paid on a monthly basis by the owner of the villa. However, it was considered customary for each of the two employees to receive a $2 tip per day from each guest for services rendered to the household. If Louise and Michele decide to observe this custom, how much will each contribute toward tips for the 30 days they will be staying at the villa? _____

More About Louise and Michele at the Villa

The villa's flower garden has gradually become a place where Louise and Michele spend much of their time. A table and chairs are set up in the garden for sitting leisurely and having coffee or meals. The two are enjoying the garden's many flower varieties and peaceful atmosphere, especially in the evenings.

Louise has decided to make a scale drawing of the garden with the possible notion of recreating something similar at her own house. The sketch will help Louise to remember the garden's many features. She borrowed a tape measure and was not surprised to find it in meters. Louise is familiar with using meters as units of measure and figures that it will make no difference to her drawing. The garden measures 20 meters in length by 12 meters in width. How many square meters in size is the villa's garden? _____

Louise has purchased some souvenirs to take home with her when she leaves the villa. She has found some beautiful glassware at a nearby village. So far she has purchased a set of hand-blown drinking glasses for the equivalent of about $42. She bought two very elegant-looking vases at a cost of $33 each. She also found a water pitcher for $28 that is an unusual shade of blue. Louise did not want to spend more than $200 on souvenirs this trip. How much more can Louise spend on souvenirs before reaching her limit? _____

Rudeness and Snobbery Abound in Old Book Shop

Mr. Snodgrass owns Old Connecticut Rare Book Shop. He is very happy in the book business. Rare and valuable books are his friends. They sit quietly on the shelves at his shop and wait for the opportunity to earn him money. More than anything else, Mr. Snodgrass enjoys finding a new "friend" at an exclusive auction or book show and then adding it to his store's shelves.

What Mr. Snodgrass does not like is "customers" in his shop. People who wander into his bookshop seldom enjoy a warm reception. Mr. Snodgrass has a select list of clients he likes to see in his shop. He looks upon all others as little better than intruders. Mr. Snodgrass has been keeping a tally of unwanted customers who have bothered him by needlessly wasting his valuable time in Old Connecticut Rare Book Shop. He sees that January brought in 39 people not on his favored-client list. February was a terrible month with 51 unwanted visitors. March was even more unbearable with 57 "customers" dropping in uninvited to browse. Mr. Snodgrass thinks that he might not have been rude enough during this period and will have to try harder the rest of the year. How many unwanted visitors came to his stuffy little shop during this three-month period? _____

One person Mr. Snodgrass is always glad to see in Old Connecticut Rare Book Shop is Mrs. Witherspoon. Mrs. Witherspoon is a very wealthy (and eligible) widow who stops by the shop every Thursday to add a book to her collection. In addition to being a good client, Mr. Snodgrass considers her quite enchanting. Assuming that the average price of a book in Old Connecticut Rare Book Shop is $125, how much has Mrs. Witherspoon spent in the 22 weeks she has been visiting the shop? _____

More About Old Connecticut Rare Book Shop

Mr. Snodgrass had an exceptionally good day on Monday. An older gentleman was waiting outside when he arrived to open Old Connecticut Rare Book Shop. Mr. Snodgrass detests having to deal with anyone before he has had a chance to brew a pot of coffee and listen to the morning classical music medley on his favorite station. But this day turned out to be a little different from the routine he normally enjoys.

Mr. Snodgrass was able to purchase a collection of 34 books from the waiting gentleman for the sum of $1,360. (Afterward he was glad he resisted his first impulse to be rude to the old fellow.) These books make up a set called the Lost and Forgotten Literature Classics, first published in the 1800s. Mr. Snodgrass is confident that the books will easily sell for $150 each. If all the books sell as he predicts, how much profit will Mr. Snodgrass make? _____

Mr. Snodgrass had a terrible shock during a recent book show. He found that four books had been stolen from one of his displays. To him, it was something like losing four good "friends" in a sudden accident. Mr. Snodgrass figured that it must have happened while he was arguing with another dealer about the boundary line for his booth space. Three of the books stolen were the same price, $188 each. The fourth book was a real treasure, an eighteenth-century medical text with some interesting sections on performing amputations and treating plague victims. It was priced at $450. How much money has Mr. Snodgrass lost, assuming that the stolen books would have sold for his asking price? _____

A Ranch Without Cowboys

The Alameda Nut Ranch is a family-owned operation, having been passed down through several generations. What is now Alameda Nut Ranch actually began as Alameda Cattle Ranch many years ago. Cattle proved to be unprofitable as well as hard on the land itself, so a change was made about 50 years ago. Nut-bearing orchards were planted on the ranch's 1,400 acres. Alameda Nut Ranch is now exclusively an agricultural operation.

The orchards include 800 acres of mature walnut trees. The walnut orchard represents the largest single source of income for Alameda Nut Ranch. The balance of land is evenly split between almond trees and pecan trees. How many acres of pecan trees are there at Alameda Nut Ranch? _____

Alameda Nut Ranch has explored a number of different recycling options for waste disposal. Massive amounts of empty nut hulls are produced as a by-product of their shelling process. For many years the ranch sought practical solutions for dealing with the hulls but often ended up paying for their removal. This posed an expensive problem before it was discovered that the empty nut hulls could be sold as an ingredient for manufacturing certain types of composite wood products. Alameda Nut Ranch also keeps hulls on hand to use as fuel in the office wood stove. Thirty-five pounds of hulls will keep the office warm for an entire day. How many days of fuel will 2,800 pounds of hulls provide? _____

More About Alameda Nut Ranch

There are a number of trees in the pecan orchard with a history of producing exceptionally high-quality nuts. Realizing that these premium nuts have a good potential for high profits, Alameda Nut Ranch has developed a select clientele for these premium nuts. Several restaurants and bakeries order these premium nuts for making desserts and baked goods. Alameda Nut Ranch just sold 115 pounds of their premium-grade, shelled pecans to a regular restaurant customer. They charged the restaurant $8 per pound for the nuts and added a delivery charge of $15. What is the restaurant's total bill for the delivered pecans? _____

To get through the busy harvest season, Alameda Nut Ranch must hire a trucking company to help transport nuts. The ranch's own trucks are too busy to handle the extra capacity during the height of the harvest. The nuts are sent out to various wholesalers, customers, and shippers. The trucking company picked up the following amounts of walnuts from Alameda Nut Ranch during the first week of harvest: 655 pounds on Monday, 621 pounds on Tuesday, 819 pounds on Wednesday, 837 pounds on Thursday, and 989 pounds on Friday. Once the walnuts have been accepted by the trucking company, it becomes responsible for seeing that the walnuts are delivered to the proper destinations. How many pounds of walnuts were transported by the trucking company during this five-day period?_____

49

Online Trader Wakes Up to Reality

Kathleen's new interest is trading stocks online. Several friends have told her that day trading is neither a hobby nor a sensible way to invest money. But Kathleen is convinced that she can make a little bit of money on each stock trade, do that a "bunch" of times per day, and end up making money. After all, those people in the television commercials are doing it!

Kathleen took $20,000 from her daughter's college fund and put it into her online brokerage account. This is what she will use to double, triple, or even quadruple her money in just a short time. Kathleen's broker charges only $9 commission per stock trade, so she feels comfortable making as many trades as needed to get in and out of the good stock deals quickly. In her first month Kathleen made 212 stock trades. How much did she pay in commissions? _____

Kathleen has had a few setbacks with her online trading. Her main problem is buying stock in companies she knows nothing about. Kathleen's friends have resisted the temptation to say "I told you so" because they know that Kathleen has already lost $5,504 in only 8 weeks of trying to day trade stocks. Kathleen herself is starting to realize that this notion of stock trading might not have been such a good idea. On average, how much money has she lost per week with her stock trading scheme? _____

Grocery Shopping Discoveries

Ted shops for groceries frequently with his mother. He has noticed that some things are sold by the pound, such as meats. Some things are sold according to a quantity involved, such as eggs. Ted has also noticed that some things are sold at a per-item price, like canned goods.

When Ted's mother heard his observation, she gave him a calculator and a pad of paper. "Why don't you try to keep up with it as we shop?" she asked him. Ted made three columns on the pad: "priced-per-pound goods," "priced-by-quantity goods," and "priced-per-item goods." Ted categorized and logged all groceries as they were placed in the shopping cart. At the end of their shopping trip, he found that "priced-per-pound goods" made up $69.77 of their groceries, "priced-by-quantity goods" made up $31.27 of their groceries, and "priced-per-item goods" made up $44.58 of their groceries. How much money was spent for this shopping trip on all categories of groceries? _____

Ted noticed that the same product is frequently offered in a number of different sizes. His mother mentioned that larger sizes were usually cheaper "per unit." Ted noticed that a 2-pound box of laundry detergent cost $3.20, while a 4-pound box of this same detergent cost $5.80. Ted thinks his mother is right about the cheaper per-unit cost of larger sizes but wants to check the figures to make certain. How much more would it cost to purchase two 2-pound boxes of detergent instead of just buying the single 4-pound box?

_____

Model Horses Make Sought-After Collectibles

Carey collects model horses. The horse models are made from plastic, poured into molds at the factory while the plastic is still in a hot liquid state. The models are then painted to denote the proper coloration for the particular breed being represented. The result is a realistic, much sought-after collectible horse model.

Carey has a large collection of these model horses. Although she has been collecting them for only four years, her collection numbers 288 horses. Carey has used her allowance every month to amass this collection. She buys a set number of horse models per month, increasing her collection in a very predictable pattern. How many models per month has Carey been buying? _____

Carey spends a great deal of time following her hobby. There are several organizations that publish newsletters and numerous Web sites that provide model horse information. Carey monitors a number of these publications in an effort to stay informed. She has recently noticed a new price trend emerging.

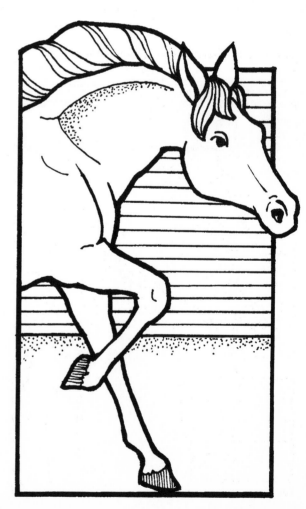

There have always been a number of companies advertising to buy these model horses on the after-market. In the past, the majority of these companies usually offered $15 for a model in "new" condition. Carey has noticed that the average bid price suddenly seems to have increased to $17 per model horse! If Carey were to sell 31 of her least favorite model horses, how much money could she expect the sale to generate if the $17 figure is accurate? _____

More About Carey's Model Horses

Carey and her mother are traveling to a nearby state to attend a convention for model horse enthusiasts. These conventions are held around the country regionally during the summer months so collectors can meet to see the new product offerings. The conventions also provide a good opportunity for collectors to trade models among themselves.

Carey has put together a small group of model horses to use as trading stock. She will trade them if she sees something she would rather have in their place. She has also managed to save $200 to use for acquiring models that are difficult to obtain through the places she regularly shops. On the first day at the convention, Carey traded away three horses and spent $91.50 from her $200 fund. How much money does Carey have left for the second day of the convention? _____

With the convention finished, Carey and her mother are headed home. Carey feels that the convention was an enormous success. She managed to acquire 9 new horse models through either trading or straight cash purchases! During the drive home, Carey has had the opportunity to do some new figuring based on the transactions she completed at the convention. She also collected a lot of pricing information at the convention pertaining to her collection back home. According to Carey's records, she has spent a total of $3,202.45 on her entire model horse collection. She thinks that her collection is now worth $4,110.50 based on what she has just learned at the convention. How much more does her collection appear to be worth beyond what she spent in acquiring it? _____

A Fool and His Money

Jonathan has always had a keen interest in sports. But his interest in sports does not include actually participating in any kind of sporting events. Jonathan is an avid collector of sports memorabilia. From the time Jonathan first began working, every spare cent he has earned has gone into expanding his sports memorabilia collection. Jonathan believes so strongly in his "collectible investments" that he has refused to participate in his company's retirement plan, instead preferring to buy collectibles with the money.

Jonathan recently paid a sports memorabilia dealer $89 for an autographed baseball card. He saw this dealer's ad in the classified section of a sports collectibles magazine. Jonathan bought the card by mail order and also had to pay a $16 shipping and handling fee. Upon receiving the card, Jonathan discovered that the autograph was a fake and returned the card to the dealer, paying a shipping charge of $4.80 to return it. Jonathan now wants a refund for the card's original price plus all the shipping charges he paid. He has returned the card and expects his refund to arrive any day now. The card was returned several weeks ago, and all Jonathan's friends are telling him that he has been hoodwinked. How much should his refund be, if it ever does arrive?

_____

Jonathan also has a collection of expensive tournament golf balls. He buys them for $15 each through the mail from a plumbing-supply company in New Jersey. Once again, Jonathan's friends have warned him that he is being duped, but Jonathan assures them that this company is a legitimate, part-time dealer in authentic sports collectibles. Jonathan's collection of golf balls is housed in a partitioned display that is 15 rows tall by 12 rows wide. The display frame is constructed so that each golf ball is contained in its own box within its row. The frame will be full when only seven more golf balls are added. How many golf balls does Jonathan currently have in this display frame?_____

More About Jonathan's Collectibles

Jonathan is taking his three nephews to
a baseball card show. The nephews had asked to tour
the art museum instead, but Jonathan thinks that the baseball card
show is a better place for young people to learn about the world around them. He will
pay admission for the nephews, and his own, too. Jonathan also plans to give each
nephew $15 to spend at the baseball card show. Admission to the show is $4.50 per
person. Jonathan expects this show to be well worth the price of admission! He also
plans to spend $200 on items for his own card collection. How much money will
Jonathan need to set aside to pay for this outing? _____

Jonathan took a hard look at his sports
memorabilia collection after he had an
independent appraiser come to his house
to evaluate the collection. The appraiser
was not affiliated with any memorabilia
dealers, so Jonathan was convinced that
the appraisal would be fair. The appraiser
valued Jonathan's collection at $2,445. This
may sound like good news, but Jonathan
had previously paid a total of $17,101 in
acquiring the collection. In disgust at his
own foolish behavior, Jonathan consigned
his entire collection to an auction house
to be liquidated. The auction house did a
good job of selling Jonathan's collection. It
was sold for slightly more than the
appraisal, $2,909. How much money has
Jonathan lost by investing in sports
memorabilia? _____

Cranky Grandfather Mellows Out

Glen has sold an expensive piece of real estate he owned near a resort on the coast. The land was doing him no good, and he wanted to do something meaningful with the money. Glen has six grandchildren, all of whom are currently in middle school or high school. Glen's grandchildren think he is both cranky and stubborn, but he does not hold this view against them since it is mostly true. That is why Glen has decided to do something nice for his grandchildren.

Glen expects to receive $199,374 from closing the sale of his property. He plans to give each grandchild an equal share of this money. Glen would like to see them use the money for something important, such as going to college or someday buying a home. How much will each grandchild be receiving? _____

Glen has been feuding with his next-door neighbor, Max, for 55 years! The two have never come to blows, but there have been many names called and pranks played by each of them over the decades. Glen and Max went to school together and were good friends at one time, so it seems silly for them to have been angry all these years. Glen cannot even remember what the original argument was about, but it had something to do with whose property a tree was on. Since the tree died over 20 years ago, Glen thinks it might be time to put the feud behind them. He has invited Max to meet him at a restaurant they both like, and he will apologize for his part in keeping the feud going all these years. If Glen was 26 when the feud began, how old is he now?

_____

Shelves of Books Used-Book Store

Shelves of Books is a used-book store. The shop carries a wide selection of genres but specializes in outdoor books. Gardening, hiking, and fishing are just a few of the more popular outdoor categories. The shop has a clientele that tends to look for these kinds of books. Lately, customers have mentioned that the store's limited hours make shopping difficult, due to the somewhat early closing times. Kim, the owner of Shelves of Books, is considering expanding the shop's business hours.

Kim wants to have the store open 2 extra hours per day Monday through Friday, and an additional 5 hours on Saturday. The shop is currently open for business Monday through Friday from 10 a.m. until 5 p.m. On Saturday the shop is open from 8 a.m. until noon. How many extra hours per week would the proposed schedule change add to the shop's current business hours? _____

Kim has also been concerned that Shelves of Books is looking a little dreary inside. It has been over 4 years since any changes were made to the store's general appearance. Kim decided that Shelves of Books needs a bit of redecorating, so she budgeted $750 to improve the overall appearance of the store. She plans to do most of the work herself, which will save on labor expenses. Kim has already spent $122.29 for paint and supplies, $136.83 for additional lighting, $202.08 for carpeting, and $77.75 for a display rack. How much money is still available in the redecorating budget after paying for these items? _____

Builder Gets Billed

Wingate Home Construction is a building company specializing in residential construction and restoration projects. Most of the houses built by Wingate are custom homes, often with special features. The restoration projects frequently involve homes originally built 60 to 100 years ago. Wingate Home Construction is currently making repairs to an 1890s-era house with four fireplaces.

The owner of Wingate Home Construction arrived at the job site early one morning to discover that there had been a break-in during the night. Vandals broke several windows and emptied paint cans onto the floor. Tools left overnight at the job site had also been stolen, including a table saw and a router saw belonging to Wingate Home Construction. The table saw will cost $339 to replace. The router saw will cost $89 to replace. But the news only got worse for the owner of Wingate Home Construction. He was also held responsible by the owner of the house for the vandalism incurred. Their contract plainly stated that no expensive tools were to be left unattended at the job site. The owner of the house maintains that it was the unattended tools that caused the break-in to occur, which in turn led to the vandalism. Fixing the broken windows and cleaning up the paint mess will cost Wingate $717. How much will this end up costing the owner of Wingate Home Construction once the tools are replaced and the mess cleaned up? _____

A former client is suing Wingate Home Construction for shoddy work done on the staircase in a restored house. The former client contends that the new staircase was not constructed to match the style of the existing architecture. The former client seeks to recover the $5,950 paid to Wingate for the work. At the urging of their own company attorney, Wingate Home Construction has offered to settle the case for half the amount sought by the former client. If the former client accepts their offer, how much money will Wingate Home Construction have to return to the former client to settle the case? _____

More About Wingate Home Construction

The owner of Wingate Home Construction is always looking for antique building materials. He frequently shops auctions, estate sales, and other such events to find the kinds of building supplies he needs for upcoming restoration jobs. Once acquired, the materials are then stored in a leased warehouse until they are needed. The owner of Wingate Home Construction recently purchased 520 antique floor tiles at an estate auction. He immediately recognized a use for these tiles when he saw them at the auction. Wingate Construction used 194 of these tiles for a restoration job the following week. The rest were stored for future use. How many antique floor tiles from the auction are still available at the warehouse for future use? _____

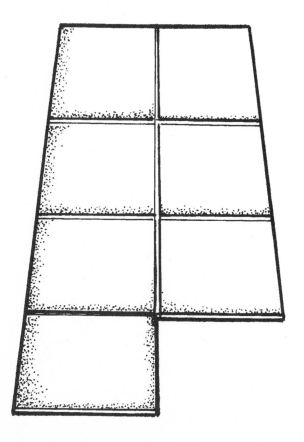

The owner of Wingate Home Construction bought a piece of land for $20,750. He often acquires potential building sites in this manner, knowing that sooner or later the land will be in demand as choice building lots. The original piece of land was later split into two lots priced at $15,500 each. Both building lots were eventually sold for the asking price as part of a house construction deal. What profit did Wingate Home Construction realize on the original land purchase? _____

Elmer the No-Nonsense Barber

Elmer owns a small barbershop. Although the shop has two barber's chairs, Elmer has worked by himself since his partner died in 1969. Elmer believes in a no-nonsense kind of haircut. He does not go in for hair styling, hair coloring, or any other kinds of "fads," as he calls them. Elmer does not sell "perfumes" (cologne), shampoo, hair gel, or any other "silly stuff" in his shop either. Anyone asking for something out of the ordinary in Elmer's Barbershop is rather curtly told that they may use Marjori's Beauty Salon next door.

Elmer charges $7.50 for a haircut. He does not offer a senior discount to people over 55. Elmer tells customers, "If a guy who is 76 years old can stand here all day cutting hair, you younger guys don't need a discount." How much money would Elmer earn in a day when he does 48 haircuts? _____

Elmer has decided to take on another barber in his shop as a junior partner. He recently explained to a friend that he was taking on the new partner by saying "got to help some of the younger folks coming up in this trade." Elmer's new partner is 61 years old.

Elmer thinks the new barber has enough experience to join his shop without needing much in the way of on-the-job training. The new partner has been cutting hair for only 43 years. Elmer has 16 more years of experience. How many years has Elmer been cutting hair? _____

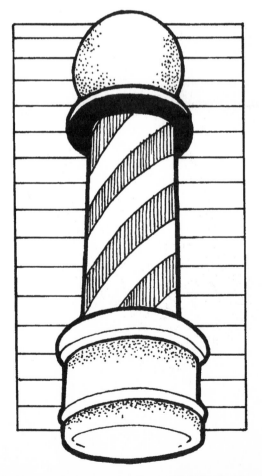

More About Elmer's Barbershop

Elmer recently threw out a door-to-door salesman. The salesman was selling a new kind of electric hair clipper that sucked up the clippings instead of just letting them fall on the floor. (This type of clipper has been on the market for over 20 years, but it was new to Elmer.) Elmer curtly told the salesman, "We don't go in for fads here at my shop, try next door."

After a time Elmer began to think that he might have made a mistake about the "new" clippers. His young partner kept hinting that the new clippers might be worth trying. If the clippers cost $219 each, how much would it cost to get one for each of them to try out? _____

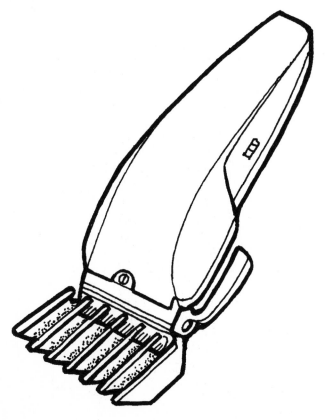

Elmer has decided to retire from the barbershop. He thinks that there are too many changes in the industry to keep up with anymore. Elmer wants to give the flower business a try. He has always kept a large flower garden at his house and thinks it might make a nice part-time business.

Elmer's new partner is willing to buy out his interest in the shop. The shop is largely a service business, but the equipment and existing customer base are worth something. The partner has offered Elmer $6,000 to take over the shop. If Elmer is to be paid in monthly installments of $200, how many months will it take the partner to completely buy out Elmer's interest in the shop? _____

Watermelon Harvest Goes Bust

Cooper has a field of watermelons ready to be harvested. With the help of a friend, he has managed to pick the watermelons and load them into a heavy truck with tall side panels. As Cooper was loading the watermelons, he kept count of them. There were 45 large watermelons, 62 medium watermelons, and 38 watermelons rather small in size.

Cooper and his friend will take the watermelons to an outdoor market and see what they can do about selling them. Cooper thinks that he will be able to get an average of $3 per watermelon when they are all sold. How many watermelons does Cooper have available to sell? _____

Cooper had a big disappointment after arriving at the market. He and his friend unloaded about half of the watermelons, then took a break. While they were taking their break, a side panel on the truck gave way, and the rest of the watermelons unloaded onto to the pavement by themselves! Many burst, completely ruined by the hard fall.

When the long day was done, the results were a bit disappointing. Cooper sold 21 large watermelons at $5 each, 29 medium watermelons at $3 each, and none of the small-sized watermelons. He had to pay a $10 fee for setting up at the outdoor market, and he had also promised his friend $25 for helping out with the harvest. How much money did Cooper end up with for his long day of effort after paying these expenses? _____

Stamp Collector Plans Acquisitions

Bonnie has been collecting stamps for several years. She has 2,290 stamps in her collection. Many of the stamps are from the United States, but most are from countries around the world.

Most of Bonnie's stamps are "used," meaning that they have been used as postage for letters or parcels. Some of those stamps have quite interesting cancellation marks. Part of Bonnie's collection is "unused," meaning that the stamps have never been used for mailing letters. Usually unused stamps are much more valuable than used stamps. That is why Bonnie has fewer unused stamps in her collection. Bonnie has 609 unused stamps in her collection; the remaining stamps are all used. How many of the stamps in her collection are used? _____

Bonnie has set aside $40.00 in her new-stamp fund to buy three new stamps for her collection. She plans to order the stamps from dealers advertising in a weekly stamp-collecting newspaper. Bonnie has located the first stamp she plans to buy. The stamp is an early airmail stamp she has been wanting to add to her collection for quite some time. It will cost $21.55 to buy this stamp plus $2.95 for shipping and handling. How much money will be left in Bonnie's new-stamp fund after this purchase is made? _____

Name _____

Furniture Gets New Coat

Amanda is planning to refurbish some of her wood furniture. She has several pieces that have been scratched or marred from moving. A couple of the pieces have also been slightly stained or have bruised spots from years of use. She plans to evaluate each piece carefully. Then she will sand, stain, and refinish the ones that most need attention.

Amanda needs a few supplies before beginning her furniture projects. One of the items she needs is wood stain. Amanda wants to find a good color of stain to apply once the wood surface has been sanded. The stain she likes is sold in two sizes. A quart of this stain costs $16.49 and a pint costs $9.99. Amanda thinks one quart plus one pint will be just enough wood stain to do all the projects. But if she is wrong and runs out, she will have to buy yet another pint of stain. If Amanda ends up needing two quarts of stain for this project, how much will she save by buying two 1-quart containers instead of buying one 1-quart container and two 1-pint containers? _____

Amanda changed her mind about buying just enough stain to complete the job when a clerk told her that a gallon of the same stain was available in the storeroom for a close-out price of $19. She decided that for the price it would be best to buy the gallon of stain and have some left over for the next project. Amanda also bought a multi-pack of paintbrushes for $12.29, a gallon of finish coat for $25.59, a pack of sandpaper at $2.29, and a drop cloth for $16. If this list represents all the supplies she needed, how much money did Amanda spend on the furniture project?

_____

More About Amanda's Furniture Project

Amanda's furniture project took much longer than she had expected, but all the pieces she refinished turned out quite well. Before beginning the work, Amanda thought that it would be interesting to keep a log of the time spent on each stage of the project. Her entries indicated the following amounts of time were spent on each stage of the project: shopping for materials, 40 minutes; sanding wood surfaces, 3 hours and 10 minutes; staining the wood, 1 hour and 20 minutes; applying finish coat, 50 minutes. How many hours did Amanda spend completing her furniture project? _____

After the furniture project was finished, Amanda began looking for other projects she might do to improve the look of her living space. One afternoon she saw a program on reupholstering couches. Amanda followed up on this idea by purchasing a book on the subject to make certain that the project was within her capabilities. Sometimes things look easier on television than they actually are.

After Amanda was confident that the upholstery project was something she could actually do herself, she went about buying materials. The biggest expense for this

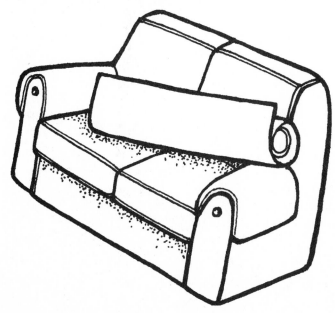

project would be the new fabric. The fabric used for couches is much heavier than that sold in sewing shops. It is also much more expensive. The fabric would have to be purchased through a home decorator, and Amanda would need an accurate figure for the amount needed to avoid wasting the expensive material. Amanda measured the couch and is certain that a piece 9 feet by 12 feet is adequate to cover the couch and make the necessary tucks. A piece this size will also provide enough material for the cushions. How many square feet of material will Amanda need for this project? _____

New Pottery, Old Look

The Pottery of Old Shop recreates pottery in the same style as it existed in years past. Pottery of Old manufactures a wide variety of historical reproductions for their product line. Typically, Pottery of Old will reproduce an antique pottery design in a strictly limited production. When that production is sold out, no further copies are made. This practice supports the prices Pottery of Old charges for its pottery, since collectors view the limited pottery runs as being more scarce and desirable.

Pottery of Old sells its pottery to the general public at its own shop. It also sells to other stores, museum shops, and upscale decorators. Pottery of Old has just finished a limited production of 400 inkwells based on a design from the 1840s. A museum store Pottery of Old frequently sells to had requested this particular design. Pottery of Old will sell 100 of these inkwells to this museum store at a special price of $18 each, since the inkwell was produced at their suggestion. Pottery of Old will sell 225 of these inkwells to other stores at a wholesale price of $22 each. The last of the inkwells will be sold through their own shop for $28 each. How much money will Pottery of Old take in from the sale of the 400 inkwells once all of them have been sold? _____

Pottery of Old has ordered 455 pounds of premium red clay from a supplier. The clay itself is costing Pottery of Old $3 per pound. This clay is a unique variety found only in the south. That is why Pottery of Old is willing to pay such a price for it. The red clay will be used to make a special edition run of clay bowls. A flat fee of $105.50 was also assessed to cover the cost of delivery. Pottery of Old has already sent its supplier a check to cover the cost of the clay and its delivery. Now they are just waiting for the shipment to arrive. How much would that check have been made out for? _____

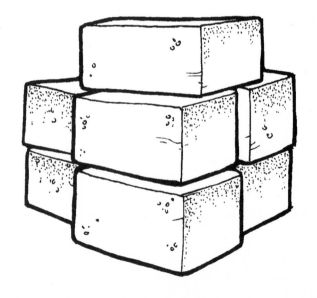

More About Pottery of Old

Pottery of Old has decided to publish a small booklet describing the pottery they make. Customers have been asking for a catalog or guidebook for quite some time. Pottery of Old figured that it was a good time for this book project to proceed, since new pottery production runs are due out soon. They have hired a writer and a photographer for the project, paying them $750 each for their services. Once the booklet is finished, it will be taken to their regular printer who is charging Pottery of Old $1,875 for the press run. Including all costs, what will Pottery of Old have spent in getting this press run of booklets completed? _____

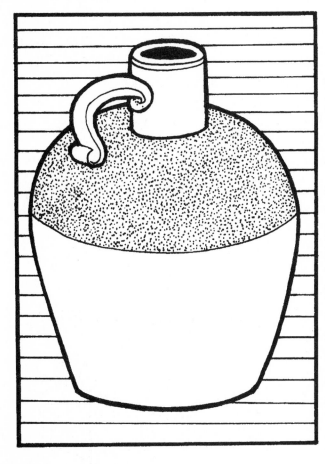

Pottery of Old has been contacted with questions about reproducing a one-quart jug used by a syrup company during the 1920s. The syrup company is still in business after all these years. It is planning to reintroduce the jug as a marketing gimmick for a new line of premium maple syrup. The jugs, filled with this new premium maple syrup, will be sold to the first 1,000 customers who place an order with the company online. Pottery of Old has quoted the syrup company a set-up charge of $1500 to begin the project, with an additional per-piece charge of $2 for each jug produced. What will the syrup company owe Pottery of Old if they go ahead with this project? _____

Travel Broadens the Person, but Not the Bank Account

Jolene is planning a trip to France over her summer vacation. Even though the trip is still months away, she is already preparing for it. She is taking a crash course in French. The class meets three days per week and costs $200 for the two months it runs. Jolene thinks that knowing a bit of the language will make travel easier.

Jolene has also paid $788.71 for her plane ticket, representing a substantially discounted advance purchase fare. She bought a travel guide for touring the French countryside for $18.99 and another for $11.49, which details only the city of Paris. Jolene still will need to arrange lodging and contend with a number of other expenses as more arrangements are made. How much money has Jolene already spent in preparing for her trip to France? _____

Jolene is now only a week from departing on her trip to France. Her itinerary includes 2 travel days and 28 days of actually touring France. All arrangements have now been made and everything is already paid for. Jolene is now trying to decide how much she needs to buy in traveler's checks for spending money and to cover minor expenses. She also wants to have the traveler's checks along in case credit cards are not accepted when she needs to buy something. For each day she is away from home, she would like to have $75 in traveler's checks. What total amount will Jolene need to get in traveler's checks to cover the amount of time she will be away? _____

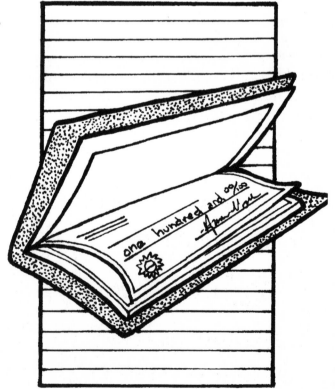

"Two" Many Chefs Spoil Everything

Henri and Rene are both chefs working at the same four-star hotel, The Grande Bellevue Resort Hotel and Convention Center. Henri and Rene do not get along well with each other. The kitchen staff is still telling the story of a disagreement between the two over how to prepare a proper chocolate dessert truffle. Anytime you have two fellows each weighing over 300 pounds jostling around like a couple of feuding walruses, it makes for a memorable event. Normally, Paul, the restaurant's manager, schedules Henri and Rene to work different shifts in an effort to keep the two apart. Occasionally, the two must work the same shift, due to vacation time being used by other employees or especially busy times for the restaurant.

Paul has scheduled Henri to come in on Saturday at 7 a.m. and work until 3 p.m. He has scheduled Rene to come in at 11 a.m. and work until 7 p.m. Paul knows that their schedules will overlap on this particular Saturday. He has asked Mira, a kitchen assistant well-liked by both chefs, to run interference between the two and keep them from quarreling. How many hours will Mira have to play the part of peacemaker for the two temperamental chefs? _____

Henri and Rene had a discussion one day after work and decided that it was Paul who had caused the chocolate dessert truffle disagreement. After all, what kind of manager assigns two accomplished chefs the exact same task? It was bound to lead to trouble. Although it was Paul's fault, Henri and Rene have decided to let bygones be bygones.

With Paul's birthday approaching, Henri and Rene are planning a special surprise. They are baking a cake. The cake will be a large sheet cake with dimensions 24 inches wide by 36 inches long. Henri will cut the cake and Rene will serve pieces to the restaurant employees. They will save a large piece of cake, 12 inches wide by 18 inches long for Paul. How many square inches of cake will Paul get to eat when the two chefs go ahead with their birthday surprise? _____

Birdhouse Builder Gets Creative

James noticed that the birdhouses on his property were looking rather decrepit. A few had even collapsed since he last checked them. When he thought about it, James realized that it had been over five years since he had made and installed any birdhouses. He decided to make this his Saturday project, since spring was quickly approaching and the houses would soon be needed.

After checking his workshop, James realized that he would need a few items to get his birdhouse project going. He purchased nails at a cost of $1.79 and lumber at a cost of $24.50. James also decided to paint the outside of the birdhouses with a water sealant to give the houses added protection against the weather. The sealant he purchased cost $8.89. How much money has James spent to get the birdhouse project going? _____

A neighbor came over just as James was beginning his birdhouse project. The neighbor mentioned a few creative ideas he had seen used on a television program for building birdhouses. One idea centered around using an expired license plate as the roof for a birdhouse. James thought this idea was especially inventive and decided to delay the start of his birdhouse project until some license plates could be purchased. He was eventually able to buy seven expired license plates at a flea market. James paid $4 per plate but thinks it will be well worth the additional expense once the license plates have been used in the project. How much money did adding this creative element increase the overall cost of his birdhouse project? _____

More About James and the Birdhouses

After James finished the birdhouses for his yard, he began thinking about replacing the duck houses down at his pond. They appeared in better overall condition, but James decided that it would be a good time to deal with them as well. After taking down the old duck houses, James decided that some of the materials could be reused. The flooring in the duck houses was made of a shelving-type board 8 inches wide. James found that the flooring in all five houses needed replacement.

James is planning to remove the front of each duck house, knock out each floor panel with a hammer, then slide in the new piece of flooring material and secure it with a few small nails. The old flooring pieces are all 10 inches long. What is the minimum length piece of wood James will need to select for the replacement flooring pieces, not counting the tiny amounts of length lost when the saw blade cuts out the pieces? _____

Months have passed and James thinks that his birdhouses are a success. He has observed six pairs of birds occupying the different houses on his property. Some of the birds are different species and, of course, have different nesting habits. James has had a hard time counting the actual offspring of each pair since he does not want to get near enough to the nests to disturb the birds. If each pair of nesting birds can raise just three chicks to maturity, how many new hatchlings will James have helped with his birdhouses?

_____

A Job Studying?

Sheila is an animal biologist. Her job is studying animals and observing their behaviors. She is frequently called upon by different agencies to conduct field observations or to offer suggestions for the conservation of animal habitats.

On a recent assignment, Sheila was called by a park official to study the aftermath of a prairie fire on a population of prairie dogs. The fire was a natural occurrence, caused by lightning strikes. Sheila had studied this prairie dog town prior to the fire and had previously estimated its population at 305 residents. Since the fire, she now estimates a population of 288 prairie dogs for the town. According to her new estimate, how many prairie dogs were lost to the fire or other causes since she last studied them? _____

Sheila wants to research a squirrel population inhabiting an island several hundred miles from her office. A colleague has written her proposing a unique theory about the special habits of this particular squirrel population. This colleague wants Sheila to participate in a joint study of these squirrels and cooperate in publishing a paper of the results.

It is a good opportunity for Sheila, but she must weigh the travel expenses in making her decision. The colleague asked Sheila to participate but did not offer to pay her travel costs. The end of the budget year is approaching and only $1,622.65 remains in Sheila's travel budget. She has produced a budget for the proposed trip, trying to reduce expenses to the bare minimum. But she figures the research trip will still cost $2,112! How much money does her travel budget lack for this proposed research trip?

More About Sheila the Biologist

Sheila has been studying nesting birds.
The site she has selected for study has 32 nesting pairs
of terns, a type of shore bird. She thinks that four pairs of the birds will
be unsuccessful in hatching any young. The other pairs should hatch two chicks each.

Sheila considers this an important nesting site due to the declining numbers of this tern variety. Sheila has decided to construct a boundary fence around the nesting birds in order to keep hikers and beach-goers from disturbing them. She will make the boundary fence in the shape of a large rectangle, using wooden stakes with a colorful tape connected between the stakes. The colorful tape will have signs attached, warning people to stay clear of the area. How many meters of tape will she need for enclosing the nesting site with a boundary fence having length of 75 meters and width of 22 meters? _____

Sheila was recently contacted by a local landowner. The landowner was concerned that an owl had taken up residence in a barn on his property. The landowner wanted to continue using this barn but also wanted the owl to feel comfortable there. Sheila evaluated the situation, making several recommendations to the landowner.

After the owl hatched its young, Sheila began driving to this farm 4 times a week to monitor the progress of this family of barn owls. The landowner has encouraged her trips and given Sheila the freedom to come and go as needed. The farm is located 22 kilometers from Sheila's office. How many kilometers per week does Sheila drive in order to monitor the owls? _____

Cooking by the Numbers

George helps his mother in the kitchen from time to time. He is not really that interested in cooking but sees the practical benefits of knowing how things are done. George's mother is preparing a pot roast for the evening meal. George has noticed that she seems to have a very orderly approach to managing the tasks involved in getting this meal started. The roast will need to cook an hour and a half. George's mother wants the roast to be done by six o'clock, when the family plans to sit down to dinner. While the roast is cooking, she will need to add the vegetables to the covered pot 45 minutes before the roast is done. What time will George's mother add the vegetables? _____

George is planning to bake a cake and a pie for a school bake sale. He wants to do most of the work himself, but his mother has agreed to watch and advise him as needed. The cake will be easier since the mix is in a box and all that needs to be added is an egg and water. The pie will be more difficult, as George is planning to make both the crust and the filling from scratch.

George's mother has suggested that the pie and the cake ideally should be baked separately so the flavors do not interfere with each other. The cake will take 45 minutes to bake. The pie will take 55 minutes to bake. George's mother also recommended that he make the cake first, since it is easier to prepare and will take only 15 minutes to mix and put into a pan. While the cake is baking, George will prepare the pie. Once the cake is done, the pie can then be put right into the oven. If George begins this project at 4 o'clock and everything goes as planned, what time will the pie come out of the oven?

Time for Everything

Amy operates a small vegetable stand during the summer months. The stand is situated in front of her parents' farm, convenient to a well-traveled highway. The stand is nothing fancy, just an open-air shed of sorts. It was built mostly from plywood and scrap materials from another project. Amy has put some effort into painting the stand and has also made signs to advertise her hours. During the summer, she typically opens the stand for 2 hours per day in the late afternoon on weekdays and for 4 hours on Saturday mornings. The stand is closed Sundays since she meets with her pony club during that time. How many hours per week does Amy operate her vegetable stand? _____

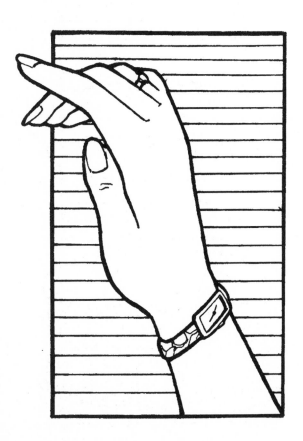

During the school year Amy keeps a very busy schedule. She has a lot of responsibilities around the farm but also manages to participate in after-school clubs. To maintain such a busy schedule, Amy must manage her time carefully. Before taking on any new obligations, she must weigh the importance of that new activity against her other interests. Amy is considering joining one of two different clubs. The Young Gardeners' Club meets after school Monday through Friday for 20 minutes per day. The Chess Club meets only on Tuesdays and Thursdays, but each meeting is 1 hour. How much time would be saved per week by joining the Young Gardeners' Club instead of the Chess Club?

_____

Survey Company Gets the Figures

The Thompson Land Survey Company provides measurements for tracts of land and confirms property lines at the request of landowners. Thompson Survey has been hired by a developer to mark off the house lots in a new development. This developer prefers the lots to be rectangular and has instructed Thompson Survey to make as many good rectangular building lots as possible, keeping the number of odd-shaped lots to a minimum.

Thompson Survey has just finished marking off the house lots, producing 14 rectangular building sites. The shape of the overall property prevented Thompson Survey from making rectangular lots from all the land involved, so 6 lots had to be laid out with irregular shapes. Thompson Survey was paid $2,800 for its work on the project plus a bonus of $100 offered by the developer for each rectangular lot that could be created. How much will Thompson Land Survey Company collect for this job? _____

Thompson Land Survey Company has just finished surveying a piece of property with six sides. The property is being evaluated for a fence, and the owner wants the property lines clearly marked. The property's sides were carefully measured and marked with painted wooden stakes by a Thompson Survey crew. Figures were double-checked back at the office to ensure their accuracy. A sketch of the property was then prepared for the owner showing the following lengths for the sides indicated on the drawing: 754.54 feet, 244.44 feet, 409.65 feet, 268.12 feet, 717.24 feet, and 238.80 feet. What is the perimeter of this piece of property? _____

More About Thompson Land Survey Company

Business has been a little slow for Thompson Land Survey Company. The local county board of supervisors has placed a restriction on new developments until a growth plan can be adopted. Even quarrels between neighbors over property lines, usually a good source of business, have been scarce lately.

Thompson Survey has supplemented its work by taking on projects it would usually consider outside its normal area of interest. The company recently laid out the boundary stakes for a pool that was being built. Another project involved setting up the lines for a new driveway. Thompson Survey has just been called in to set up a rectangular patio behind a house. The patio will be 18 feet wide by 34 feet long. The property owner, not really a "math person," wants to know how many square feet of space that will be once the patio is built. What figure will Thompson Survey supply to the owner? _____

Business may be picking up again for Thompson Land Survey Company. One of their old clients has just died. This client owned a 212-acre farm previously surveyed by the Thompson Company. The property is to be split among four heirs, who will each get a piece of this property based on a drawing and description left by the owner and witnessed by his lawyer.

After studying the drawing and the written instructions, Thompson Survey began marking off the new property lines. One heir will get 44 acres of good pasture land. Another heir gets the house and 9 acres around the house. A 55-acre plot of standing timber has been left to another heir. A large swamp covers the remaining portion of the property and was earmarked for the fourth heir. How many acres of swamp land will this heir receive? _____

The Surest Way to Make Money in Art

Angie is the manager of Messy Brush Art Store. Her duties include ordering inventory for the store, supervising employees, and assisting customers with selections. Several artists who regularly shop at Messy Brush Art Store have told Angie about a local property owner who might be a source for pottery-making clay. It seems that this landowner has a high-quality natural clay deposit on his property. Many artists in the area are eager to try this clay. It is a special variety sought by a number of Angie's customers.

After a favorable talk with the landowner, Angie arranged for the purchase of 109 pounds of clay. She waited until the clay was actually delivered to the store before deciding how it would be packaged. The clay was then separated into blocks weighing 4 pounds each and wrapped in plastic to keep it moist. Since the clay was a new product for the store, Angie figured that the 4-pound packages would give customers enough clay to judge its qualities without having to buy a lot of material. Assuming that all of the clay is useable, how many 4-pound blocks of clay will Angie be able to make from the 109-pound batch of clay? _____

Messy Brush Art Store stocks a large variety of art supplies. This includes paints, pastels, marker pens, and colored pencils. The colored pencils are often favored by those not experienced with other mediums, particularly beginning art students. Messy Brush Art Store sells colored pencils both in sets and individually.

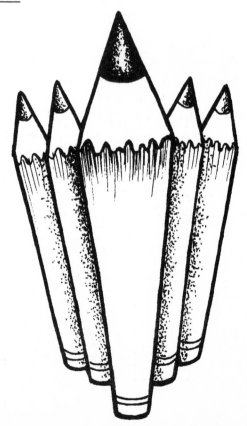

Customers may purchase colored pencils individually for $1 each, or they can buy 5 colored pencils for $4. The "5 for $4" deal represents a slight discount for buying the colored pencils in quantity, but the discounted price is good only on multiples of five. Colored pencils not purchased in groups of five are considered to be singles, and the regular price of $1 is applied. How much would it cost to purchase 18 colored pencils at Messy Brush Art Store? _____

More About the Messy Brush Art Store

Angie periodically arranges for various local artists to conduct workshops through Messy Brush Art Store. The workshops cover a wide array of topics from beginner to advanced level. Angie figures that it is a good way to promote interest in art. She also figures that people who are taking these workshops will need to buy art supplies!

Eight students have signed up for a watercolor workshop offered by the Messy Brush Art Store. This particular workshop is geared toward more advanced students and will focus on landscape techniques. The students are paying $45 each to attend the one-day workshop. Messy Brush Art Store collects the tuition money as students sign up for the workshop. Angie has selected a local artist noted for landscapes to conduct the workshop. How much will Messy Brush Art Store have left of the tuition money after paying this local artist $200 to teach the workshop? _____

Messy Brush Art Store offers a delivery service to several of its more valued customers. Usually, these customers are artists who use a large amount of supplies, but sometimes deliveries will be made to a school or studio needing supplies for special classes or events. Normally, a customer ordering supplies for delivery will purchase more than just a few items, since a fee is charged for this delivery service.

A regular customer has placed a telephone order for 35 tubes of paint from Messy Brush Art Store. The customer also wants 20 sheets of heavyweight art paper costing $4 per sheet. The paint ordered costs $7 per tube. A flat fee of $20 will be charged for delivering the supplies to the customer's address. What should the customer be billed for this order? _____

Furniture Shopping Made Easy

Reggie has been shopping for a new couch and a coffee table. His old coffee table was recently destroyed when a very heavy friend fell on it during a party. The table was smashed beyond repair, but they got some use out of the pieces for fireplace kindling. The strong smell coming from Reggie's couch after the party made it destined to go as well. Since there was no safe way the couch could also be burned in the fireplace, Reggie wisely put it out on the curb to be picked up on the next trash day.

Reggie knows exactly what he is looking for in a couch. It must be stain resistant, yet stylish at the same time. The coffee table must also be stylish. (And able to withstand his 400-pound best friend falling on it, if it should ever happen again.) Reggie's only other constraint for the couch and coffee table is that they must not cost him more than $199 combined. Reggie has found a couch he likes at a local thrift store for $99.99, but he is hesitant to buy it without first considering his overall furniture budget. If he buys this couch, how much will be left in his furniture budget for getting a heavy-duty coffee table? _____

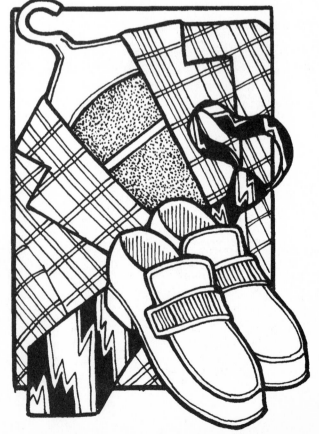

While Reggie was at the thrift store, he noticed that a number of perfectly good men's suits in his size had been donated! The suits are of a style that was popular in the 1960s. Reggie thinks that the suits have a "retro" look, currently very popular among fashionable people. He has decided to give four of the suits a try. Reggie especially likes a plaid suit he picked out that reminds him of the outfit worn by a famous country western singer of the 1960s. The thrift store charges $8 per suit regardless of the size or style. Reggie has also selected a pair of shoes for $5 and two neckties at $3 each. What will Reggie owe for the clothing items he has selected? _____

Factory Tour Astounds Visitors

Amelia and her mother are touring a factory. The factory is actually a processing facility for the Green Valley Cheese Company. Cheeses are both produced and packaged at this facility.

On the day of their visit, Green Valley Cheese Company was processing a large run of extra-sharp, smoked cheddar cheese. Amelia and her mother were astounded at the company's large vats and mechanized operations. Much of the facility was run by computer-monitored equipment. Even packaging the cheese was accomplished entirely by machines. Amelia heard the tour operator mention that four 1-pound blocks of cheese were produced each minute the factory line was running. If the production line were running the entire time, how many pounds of cheese would have been produced during the 20 minutes Amelia and her mother were touring the Green Valley Cheese Company's processing facility? _____

Before their visit to the Green Valley Cheese Company, Amelia's mother gave her $20 to spend however she wanted. Amelia stopped at the factory outlet gift store after the tour and purchased a Green Valley Cheese sampler pack for $11.99 to give to her grandmother. She also bought an insulated plastic drinking mug for $2.79. She paid with the money her mother had given her before the tour. How much of her money would still remain after Amelia made these purchases? _____

Bus Ride Means Big Drain on Time

Claire lives way out in the country. Her bus stop is one of the last stops on the route. The bus driver lives just a short distance down the road from her own house, so Claire is one of the first riders picked up in the morning and among the last dropped off in the afternoon. She has noticed that riding the bus to school takes 38 minutes in the morning. Because of traffic and the slightly different route used in the afternoon, it takes her 46 minutes to get home. Claire is not able to do anything productive during this time, as she gets queasy if she tries to read or work on schoolwork. She has decided that the only thing to be done with the time is to listen to news or radio programs on her portable radio. How many hours per week is she spending on these bus rides? _____

Claire was surprised to get home from school on her birthday to find her father busy building her a playhouse. Claire had long wanted a place of her own to go, free from intrusions by her two brothers. This was the best birthday gift she could possibly have hoped for!

By the time she got home, the playhouse foundation and flooring were already set up in the backyard near the rose garden. Her father was in the process of raising the sides of the playhouse. Claire was eager to do a bit of planning. Her father told her that the interior dimensions of the playhouse would be 5 feet by 9 feet once the playhouse was finished. How many square feet of floor space does this give Claire to work with? _____

Name _____

More About Claire's Projects

Claire has been helping her father construct a wooden fence around a small area they intend to turn into a horse paddock. Since the fence will be made of solid wood posts and boards, it will be much more expensive than the wire fence they normally use for other areas of the property. Her father has spent a total of $350 on wood and supplies for this project. The area to be enclosed is a rectangle 20 feet by 15 feet. How much per foot will this paddock fence cost if no other materials are needed for completing the project? _____

Claire has been raising quail with the intention of selling them when the birds reach maturity. She has done this before and has enjoyed some financial success with the endeavor. All of the birds in the last group she raised sold on a single Saturday after being advertised!

Claire already had most of the equipment needed for getting started, such as incubators for the eggs and pens for when the chicks hatched out. Claire kept a very careful record of her expenses. She paid a company $36 for the eggs and a shipping charge of $8. Food mash for the quail cost $18. Claire was pleased with how well the birds did. When it was time to sell the birds, she spent $3 for a marker and poster to make a sign for advertising the birds. What was Claire's total cost to get the quail ready to market? _____

Local Television Show Fixes It Up!

Steven produces a home improvement and gardening program for a local television station. The 1-hour program, called **Fix-It-Up,** is aired on Saturday afternoons. **Fix-It-Up** is built around taking a small crew out to a pre-selected home site and making improvements over the course of a couple of days. The projects are varied each week to keep viewers interested. Projects may include indoor remodeling, interior decorating, outside construction, landscaping, gardening, or any related activity that Steven thinks would be of interest to viewers. Viewers may write in with suggestions for program topics, and Steven personally screens these letters for suitable project ideas.

After a project has been selected, Steven meets with the homeowner to evaluate the site and schedule a convenient time for shooting the **Fix-It-Up** segments. Part of Steven's job is making the homeowner aware of budget limitations. The station will allow Steven to spend only $1,500 to produce each episode of **Fix-It-Up.** Within that amount, materials must be purchased and all other expenses paid. For the coming year Steven has been asked to produce 26 episodes of **Fix-It-Up.** How much is his total budget for the coming year? _____

Steven has decided to do a tile project for the next episode of **Fix-It-Up.** A number of viewers have written in suggesting a tiling project, and Steven thinks that it will make a good program. After visiting the intended project site and taking measurements, Steven figures that the ceramic tile for this project will cost $779. How much money will be left of this episode's $1500 budget after the tile is purchased? _____

More About the Fix-It-Up Show

Steven has decided to depart from the regular **Fix-It-Up** program format. Ordinarily, each episode covers a new topic with a new home site involved. Steven has been considering an idea sent in by a viewer for a multi-episode project involving the renovation of a pier and its attached boathouse. This seems like a good idea to Steven, since there are a number of large lakes in the area, and many of the station's viewers undoubtedly own boats.

Steven will combine three 1-hour episodes to fully cover the pier and boathouse renovation project. How many total minutes of viewing time will be spent on the boathouse renovation episodes? _____

Fix-It-Up has had a very good season so far. The show's popularity has seen a dramatic increase. The station's manager gave Steven $5,100 with instructions that each of the season's last six episodes of **Fix-It-Up** should get an equal share of this money as an increase to the regular $1,500 budget. The manager has also hinted that **Fix-It-Up** will be continued next season with an even larger budget. How much money is being added to the budget of each episode of **Fix-It-Up** as the show finishes its season? _____

Coffee Shop Brews Good Business

The Corner Coffee Shop is located at the edge of a residential area next to the business district. It does a good trade in the morning and at lunchtime with customers who work in nearby businesses. People who live nearby tend to drift in for drinks in the evening. They often gather in small groups to sit in the shop's outside café.

Corner Coffee Shop sells not only a variety of coffee-based drinks, but also serves a limited food menu. The food menu includes sandwiches for the lunch traffic but is mostly built around rolls and doughnuts. Specialty coffee beans and related kitchen products are also offered for sale. On a busy morning, the shop had 132 customers in a 3-hour span! On average, how many customers per hour would this figure represent? _____

The manager of Corner Coffee Shop has received a number of requests for Hawaiian-grown coffee. He has decided to give it a try in the shop and has arranged to order six 50-pound bags of Hawaiian coffee beans. The coffee, at a wholesale price, will cost Corner Coffee Shop $4 per pound. A shipping charge of $18 per 50-pound bag will also be applied. What is Corner Coffee Shop's total cost for the Hawaiian coffee order? _____

More About Corner Coffee Shop

The manager at Corner Coffee Shop has set the shop's prices to be competitive with other coffee shops. The prices are also at a level that allows a good profit to be made. The shop's Special Blend coffee costs Corner Coffee Shop $3.60 per pound. The Special Blend sells for $6.89 per pound. Corner Coffee sells large lattes for $3.25 each. The manager has figured that the shop's cost to make a large latte is only $.59 each. If a customer orders two large lattes and a pound of the Special Blend coffee, how much profit will Corner Coffee Shop make on this purchase? _____

A careless customer spilled an extra large coffee on a magazine rack at Corner Coffee Shop. The customer then claimed that it was not his fault, since the cup containing the coffee was too hot when first passed to him by the employee. Corner Coffee Shop's manager figured that the spill was not worth the bother of arguing about. He also replaced the customer's coffee with a new one. Unfortunately, the eight magazines in the magazine rack were ruined by the spilled coffee. The magazines cost Corner Coffee Shop $1.50 each. How much money will it cost Corner Coffee Shop to replace the ruined magazines? _____

Tortoise Races Bore Audience

Mike and Albert each have several pet tortoises. They like their pets well enough, but the tortoises are a bit less interesting than they had hoped for. Mike had the idea of building a short course, a racetrack of sorts for their tortoises. The two could match up their pets on the track and have the benefit of seeing some exciting competition when the tortoises race each other for the finish line.

Mike and Albert have been playing up their idea around their neighborhood. The two have nearly completed the track they will use for racing the tortoises. The track is actually just a dirt course they have supplemented with a few boards to keep the tortoises on track. They have spent only $4.50 so far to get the track finished and their idea moving forward. The two even managed to sell nine $2 admission tickets to their opening event. After expenses are taken out, how much money are they ahead so far on their tortoise racetrack idea? _____

Mike and Albert had a setback upon opening their tortoise racetrack. Several patrons of the event complained bitterly of boredom after the first scheduled race took over 20 minutes to complete. One patron mistakenly insisted that a tortoise participating in the event was dead and wanted a refund for being sold a ticket to "watch a funeral procession for a tortoise."

Mike and Albert put their heads together and quickly came up with a plan to save their opening day. They served soft drinks and chips in an effort to keep patrons happy while the races played out. After the race was finished, Mike made an offer to each of the four patrons who had not already left. The four would receive season passes to the tortoise races if they would each agree to sell three $2 tickets to the next race event. How much money will this generate for Mike and Albert if all the tickets are sold? _____

Too Many Laptop Computer Choices

Kurt has been thinking of buying a laptop computer. He does not really do a lot of traveling but thinks the convenient size of a laptop would make using it in different parts of his house easier. Kurt especially likes the notion of working on a laptop while comfortably lying in bed or on the couch. (Friends tell Kurt that he needs to get out more.)

Kurt has narrowed his search to a company that makes laptops according to the features you request when you place your order. The basic price of the computer he is considering is $1,799. Kurt will upgrade the memory for $99 and order an extra battery for $69. He will also order a travel bag for the laptop at $49, in case he decides to follow his friends' advice about getting out more. How much money will Kurt's laptop end up costing? _____

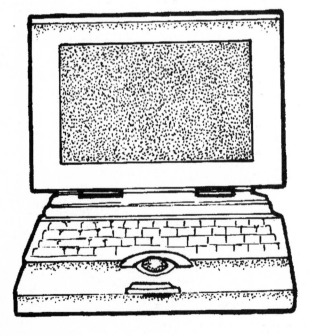

Kurt is considering buying a deluxe warranty for his computer. The laptop comes with a 1-year warranty that covers basic parts and labor for repairs. Under that warranty the customer must pay for the computer to be shipped back to the company's repair facility. The customer also has to do without the computer while it is being fixed. The deluxe warranty Kurt is considering costs $180 but has many features not offered under the free warranty.

The deluxe warranty covers three years and guarantees the customer next-day service in his or her own home. A replacement computer will be loaned to the customer free of charge if the laptop cannot be repaired on-site the very next day. Kurt thinks that this sounds like a pretty good deal. How much money does the deluxe warranty work out to per month?

_____

Publisher Takes New Approach

Wild West Publishing Company prints books and other materials related to the Old West. Subjects have included books on gold mining, ghost towns, and tales of Old West outlaws. This narrow strategy has been quite successful for them in the past. Recently, a new editor at Wild West Publishing, Gail, decided to shift from this successful format into other areas. She saw a potential for growth in areas previously ignored by Wild West Publishing. Gail began looking at manuscripts on western cooking, square dancing, western folk songs, and poetry collections by western writers.

The owner of Wild West Publishing Company got wind of Gail's new strategy and called her in for a meeting. He was initially very disturbed by the new titles she had planned but decided to give her ideas a try after she fully explained the profit potential of the new titles. As an example, Gail used a cookbook she was planning to publish. This cookbook on edible plants and reptiles would be printed at a cost of $3.19 per book on an initial press run of 5,000 copies. Gail pointed out that the cookbooks would be sold to bookstores for $5 each. How much profit per book does this represent? _____

Bill, nicknamed Wild Bill by the other employees in the print room, was Wild West Publishing's chief printer. Bill is a person easily given to impulsive behavior. (That is the reason for his nickname.) When he heard that the company would soon begin printing cookbooks and poetry collections, he flew into a rage and quit without notice during the middle of a big print job. Wild Bill wanted no part of the new line of books, explaining that he had a reputation to protect. The print room assistants can manage some of his work, but they are unable to process the more complicated jobs. The delay in press runs will cost Wild West Publishing $835 per day. How much money will Wild West Publishing lose if it takes eight days to find a new chief printer? _____

More About Wild West Publishing Company

Mason, another editor at Wild West
Publishing Company, is considering some new book
projects. He does not believe in folk songs, poetry collections, or books
with creative recipes for eating lizards. Mason wants to publish a book about a
previously unknown but very vicious Old West outlaw. He thinks that this particular
outlaw committed enough notorious jailbreaks to provide material for a good book.
Mason has $38,650 left in his budget for acquiring the rights to unpublished book
titles. He knows that it usually costs $7,500 to acquire the rights to a book title and
pay for a small press run on the book. Mason is even considering doing a series on this
outlaw if sales look promising after the first book is published. How many book titles
would the budget allow Mason to consider at this time? _____

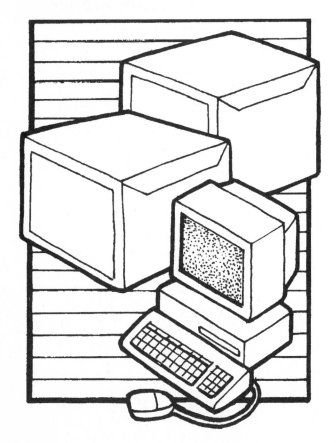

Wild West Publishing is buying 20 new computers for its editorial staff. (The owner of Wild West Publishing has decided that Mason will not be on the list to receive one of these new computers.) The new computers will come equipped with special software for developing projects and providing financial analysis as the projects go into production. The company selected to provide the computers will also set them up on-site as part of the deal. The new computers will cost $1,400 each, but the company selling them will deduct $175 for each of the old computers used as a trade-in. What will Wild West Publishing owe for the new computers if 16 of the old computers are used as trade-ins? _____

Getting the Course in Shape

Andrew is the greenskeeper at North Meadows Golf Course. Spring is fast approaching and there are numerous things he needs to do to get the course back into playing condition. The club members have high expectations for the course, so Andrew must be very attentive in his work, especially in treating the putting greens. During the winter the grass mostly died out; what grass was left is in poor shape. Andrew is ordering a special fertilizer mix for the greens at North Meadows Golf Course. He figures that each green will need 165 pounds of the fertilizer mix once the new grass has had a chance to get established. To treat 18 greens, how much fertilizer should Andrew order? _____

A dead tree on the tenth hole has been losing a lot of limbs. It has finally reached the point of posing a safety hazard and must be removed. Andrew figures that the total job will take 20 hours to perform. This includes cutting down the tree and removing it from the site. The stump will also have to be extracted and new sod planted over the spot. North Meadows' club manager insists that the job be completed in a single 8-hour workday, since #10 must be closed for play on the day the tree is to be cut down. He is concerned that the tree removal will turn into a drawn-out event and the club's members will blame him for the inconvenience. Andrew has assured the manager that the job will be completed in just one day. How many workers should Andrew put on this job to have it completed in a single 8-hour workday?

_____

Name _____

More About the North Meadows Golf Course

Andrew has noticed that there are several sites on North Meadows Golf Course which seem to be washing out excessively whenever there are heavy rains. He thinks that this problem could be solved by placing straw bales in strategic spots. The bales would redirect the flow of water away from more sensitive areas. Andrew has made sketches of the course showing the worst spots and how the bales should be arranged. His crew will use these sketches to carry out the work. Andrew plans to address this drainage problem in a more substantial way in the future but figures that the bales are a good way to deal with the problem for now. He has arranged to purchase 315 bales of straw. North Meadows is paying $4 per bale for the straw. What is the total cost for the straw bales? _____

North Meadows Golf Course is replacing all its gasoline-powered carts with electric carts. It is a good long-term move, since the gasoline carts are expensive to maintain and they give off bothersome fumes as well. Instead of making the change gradually as the carts wear out, the club management has chosen to do it all at one time. A date has been set after which gas carts will no longer be used. Andrew has been asked to figure the resale value of the old carts and turn in a total estimate of their value to the budget committee. There are 72 gasoline-powered carts in North Meadows' cart inventory. Twenty-two of these carts are in excellent condition and should bring about $1,200 each. Fifteen of these carts have severe mechanical problems, making them essentially worthless. The rest of the carts are in average condition and should bring $550 each. What will Andrew's estimate be for the budget committee? _____

Name _____

Saving Time, Saving Money

Jeff is working on building a deck for his house. He has also promised to build his children a tree house once the deck is finished. Jeff is trying to figure out how long it will take him to drive the nails when building these projects. He is considering the purchase of a nail gun instead of doing the job with just a hammer. A nail gun would make the work go faster and also save a lot of physical effort.

Jeff thinks that it will take him 1 hour 15 minutes to hammer nails on the deck project and 25 minutes on the tree house project. He thinks that a nail gun would allow him to do the deck in just 15 minutes and all the tree house nailing in just 5 minutes. How much time would Jeff save overall on these projects if he does buy the nail gun?

_____

Jeff's wife, Annie, thinks he is crazy for even thinking about buying a nail gun. It would just sit in the garage unused once the two pending projects were finished. Once Jeff's buddies started borrowing it, the nail gun would eventually end up broken or lost.

Annie has given Jeff permission to buy a new hammer, though. Jeff selected a Crafty Steel Model #1455. This model is also called the Construction Boss by people in the trade. It is forged steel with a synthetic bonded plastic handle. The retail price on this particular hammer is $45.99, but one of Jeff's friends is in the hardware business and can get it for $38. How much money is Jeff saving by buying this hammer through his friend? _____

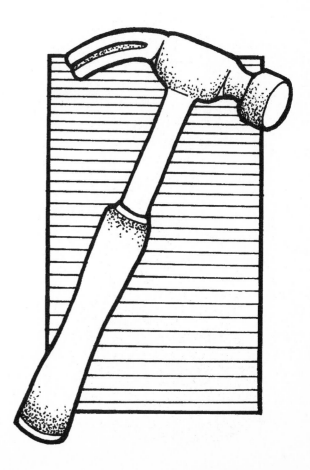

Country Retirement Gets Busy

Thomas lives out in the country. He was sitting on his porch one morning recently and noticed that the quiet road he lives on was suddenly getting an awful lot of traffic. Then a neighbor came by to tell him that another road nearby had been closed; the detour was routing people to the road they both lived on. That was fine with Thomas; since he retired there has not been much to do except sit on the porch and watch things.

Thomas decided that it might be amusing to count the cars passing by his property. In the first hour he counted 54. In the second hour the number soared to 86. The third hour brought 80 cars past his house. In the fourth hour the passing cars dropped to 48. On average, how many cars passed by Thomas's house per hour during this 4-hour span? _____

While the detour is still in effect, Thomas has decided to take advantage of all the new traffic passing by his house. He has just finished picking up the pecans produced by several trees on his property. Instead of taking the nuts to a commercial buyer, Thomas has decided to set up a little stand by the road and see if the motorists from this increased automobile traffic have any interest in buying pecans. He has packaged twelve 5-pound bags of pecans and twenty-four 2-pound bags of pecans for sale. Thomas will price the pecans at $3 per pound. On the first day, all the pecans sold except three of the 2-pound bags. How much money did Thomas take in from the pecan sales? _____

The Treetop Land, Timber, and Fur Company

In its company brochure, the Treetop Land, Timber, and Fur Company identifies itself as "an earth-friendly company interested in utilizing nature's important vast resources." Company spokespeople are quick to point out that the "Fur" portion of their company's name dates back to trapping interests of the 1800s and is no longer applicable to the company's current operations. Environmental groups familiar with Treetop's land-management practices call the company "an exploiter and pillager of irreplaceable old-growth forests and important animal habitats."

Treetop Land, Timber, and Fur Company has announced plans to clear-cut a 2,000-acre tract of land it owns adjacent to a popular national park. The trees will be sold for lumber and pulp. The land has already been slated for development. A company spokesperson was quoted as saying, "The land will be developed into a resort lodge with concessions and plenty of paid parking. Patrons wishing to use our company's facilities will be able to enjoy a natural setting with fabulous views." One environmental group has estimated that there are 28 mature trees per acre on average for this particular tract of land. How many trees would there be on the entire tract of land if the 28 trees per-acre estimate is correct? _____

Treetop Land, Timber, and Fur Company has been fined $10,000 for destroying the nest of a bird on the endangered species list. The nest was located in a tree cut down by a Treetop logging crew. A company spokesperson was quoted as saying, "We regret the inconvenience caused by this unintentional mistake. Some of our people are looking for a zoo where these displaced animals can be taken." A law student volunteering with an environmental group has done a bit of research on Treetop Land, Timber, and Fur Company. It turns out that this is the forty-second time the company has had to pay a $10,000 fine for violating environmental laws. How much money does that represent for all 42 fines? _____

More About Treetop Land, Timber, and Fur Company

A very rich and eccentric billionaire has purchased enough stock in Treetop Land, Timber, and Fur Company to gain complete control of the company. Once in charge, the quirky billionaire fired the company president and 23 company vice presidents, saying that he "did not want a bunch of slimy crooks working for him." Company security guards helped the former executives pack the contents of their desks because the new owner was concerned about "the possible petty theft of office supplies."

The new owner has also changed the company name to Treetop Tourism and Outdoor Experiences. The company's new focus will be providing guided tours and planned outdoor activities such as camping, hiking, etc. A moratorium has been placed on logging activities, and former logging crews are undergoing new training to learn friendly guiding skills. The new owner has been running some financial projections and expects to sell 2,500 tour packages the first year. He expects to sell 7,100 tour packages during the second year. Growth is expected to explode in the third year, so no figures have been projected. If tour packages are sold for $1,500 each, how much more money will Treetop Tourism and Outdoor Experiences earn in the second year of tours than the first? _____

Treetop Tourism and Outdoor Experiences is also trying to purge all of its heavy equipment. This may prove a difficult task, as all this machinery was very expensive when first purchased. The new owner has made it clear to the sales force to take a loss if necessary to get rid of "that destructive junk." The company needs to sell 197 bulldozers, 374 log-carrying trucks, 122 dump trucks, 67 lift cranes, and 3 tractors formerly used for planting trees. How many pieces of heavy equipment have to be sold? _____

Movie Buff Produces Own Film

Kent is disappointed with the quality of programming he sees on television. He has a notion that he could put together something worth watching, perhaps for cable access or a small local network. Kent has invited several of his friends to meet with him at his house to discuss the idea of producing some kind of film or other type of original programming.

The meeting at Kent's house went very well. Five of his friends showed up, and the idea of producing a play was eventually settled upon. One of the group had already written a short play, which everyone found acceptable. The only matter left to decide was the handling of expenses. An overall budget of $1,350 was agreed upon, with the understanding that each person would contribute equally. How much money will each project member be putting into the project's budget? _____

Kent has arranged to rent a digital camera. The group will use this camera to film the play they are producing. The camera will cost $17 per day to rent. Kent thinks that it will take no more than 24 days to shoot the play. The group must hold to a strict schedule if the 24-day figure is to be met. If Kent is right, how much money out of the original $1,350 budget is available for other things after money is set aside to pay for the camera rental? _____

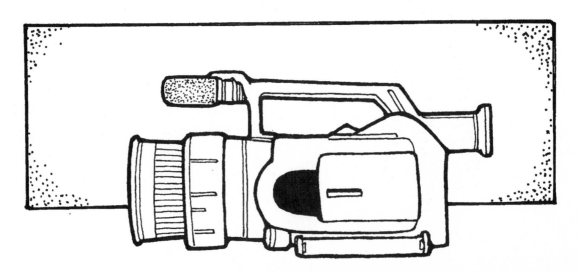

Name _____

More About Kent's Production

Kent has arranged with a local theater guild to interview actors for the film production. Even though members of the group are starring in the play's major parts, a few additional actors are still needed. The actors chosen to appear in the play understand that the film is a very low-budget production. They have agreed to work for $29 each per day. Of the three actors involved, one is needed for four days. The other two actors will be needed on the set for only three days each. How much money from the overall project should be set aside to pay for the actors? _____

Kent and his group finished shooting their play on schedule and managed to stick to the original budget as well. After the play was edited, they began showing it at Kent's house. First, they invited just a few friends not originally involved with the production. Then word began to get around that the group's production was pretty good. More people wanted to see the play. Someone with connections to a local television station even asked to see the play. The person was invited to attend a weekend showing at Kent's house.

Now the group must make a decision. A local television station has offered $2,700 to purchase the rights to the play. If Kent's group decides to accept this offer and split the money equally among the original six members of the project, how much will each person receive? _____

Wrestling Matches No Place For Reluctant Fan

Connie and her father have tickets to a wrestling event at the Mega-Dome Memorial Sports Arena. Connie's father watches wrestling programs on television each week and is very committed to following his favorite sport. Connie is not entirely certain that this event is something she will enjoy, but her father has already purchased the tickets. She feels obligated to go along since he is so enthusiastic about it. Their tickets were purchased at a cost of $22 each. Parking at the arena will cost $7. How much will the wrestling event cost them if no other expenses are incurred during the course of the evening? _____

After the wrestling event was finished, Connie concluded that the evening spent at the Mega-Dome Memorial Sports Arena was a total waste of her time. She was also more than a little disappointed at having missed her regular music lesson.

Connie was amazed at the number of people in attendance at the wrestling event. She heard the ringside announcers mention over the arena's broadcast system that paid attendance for the event was 44,415 people. Connie realized that if all of the people in attendance had paid the same $22 each for their tickets, the promoters took in an incredible amount of money. Assuming that everybody in attendance did pay $22 for their tickets, how much money did the promoters take in for the wrestling event? _____

Bulk Mailings Mean Lots of Planning

Barry has developed a new product. He plans to market this product by using bulk mailings. Barry will package brochures and send them to people on the mailing list in hopes of convincing them to buy his product. Barry's mailing list was purchased for $500 from a company that went bankrupt from selling products similar to the product Barry intends to market.

Barry has also purchased $300 in envelopes and $3,300 in postage stamps. His brochures are still being printed but will cost $1,675 when they are ready to be picked up at the printer. How much money will Barry have spent in getting the brochures mailed out by the time all expenses associated with the mailing have been paid? _____

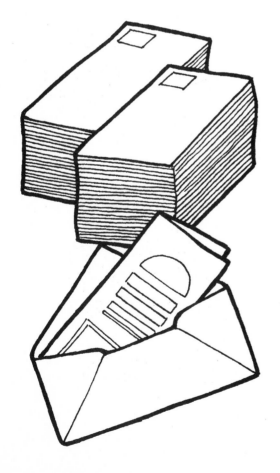

Barry sent out his brochures. He mailed all 1,000 of them on the same day and then waited for orders to come pouring in. Weeks passed and orders trickled in very slowly. This gave Barry cause for concern, as he was expecting sales to be brisk once people found out about his product.

After two months had passed, Barry had taken in only 21 orders. The orders totaled $590. Unfortunately Barry spent $9,800 altogether, developing his product and marketing it. If no more orders come in, how much money has Barry lost trying to make a business out of his product? _____

Newspaper Route Proves Profitable

Skip has been delivering newspapers for three years. In fact, he has just finished his third year on the job. He likes to think he is pretty good at it after having put in so much time with the job. His delivery route takes him through his own neighborhood and along an adjacent street, so he knows the route by heart.

Skip is outside at 4 a.m. sharp to receive his newspaper delivery. A truck drops the papers off at the curb in front of his house. Skip then takes the newspapers into the garage to roll them up and put a rubber band on each one. On rainy or snowy days, Skip has to put a plastic sleeve on each paper as well. Skip delivers all the papers by 6 a.m. and then gets ready for school. If it takes Skip 20 minutes on average to roll the newspapers and rubber-band them, how long does he take making the deliveries? _____

Skip has saved every bit of money he ever made making newspaper deliveries. He has other sources of spending money and does not want to disturb his newspaper delivery money. Skip has been paid $25 per week by the newspaper publisher for each of the 156 weeks he has been delivering newspapers. Skip has also received tips from the customers on his route totaling $274 to date. How much money has Skip made from his newspaper delivery route including both wages and tips? _____

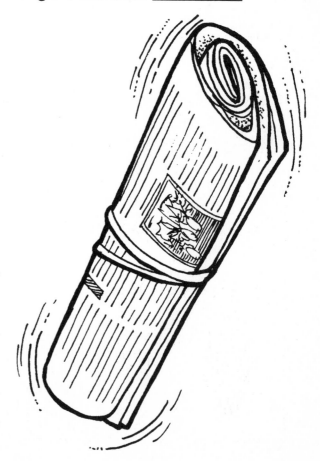

More About Skip's Newspaper Route

Skip was thinking about his newspaper route and realized that it was really just a huge rectangle. His own house is on a corner of that rectangle. Skip's regular direction of travel when delivering newspapers first takes him south of his own house. He travels six blocks and then turns west. Skip goes west for four blocks before turning back north. He continues north making deliveries and eventually turns east on the road his own house is on. Once Skip has made deliveries to the houses along the exterior of this large rectangle, he then covers all the interior streets until the deliveries are done. How many square blocks are covered by Skip's newspaper delivery area? _____

Skip is planning to give up his newspaper route for a better-paying opportunity but has offered to help his younger brother take over the route. There is quite a lot to teach him, since the job is much more than just riding a bike up and down streets throwing out newspapers.

Skip needs to make collections this afternoon on his route and figures it is a good time for his brother to learn that part of the job. He has given his brother a list of 40 houses to visit. Skip gave his brother $10 to use for making change and instructed him to collect $8 from each subscriber on the list. Skip told his brother that he should introduce himself as the new carrier-in-training to get off to a good start with the customers and that he could keep any tips collected. How much money does Skip's brother need to turn in to him once all the collections are made? _____

New Copier Decision Means Lots to Consider

Denise has been asked by her company to select new copiers for the various offices involved. Each office seems to have its own special needs in a copier. Some of the offices simply want machines capable of producing a high volume of copies. Other offices need color copies or machines capable of stapling and binding. Denise must weigh all of these requests against the budget money available and the priority that has been assigned to each office. The priority list determines which offices are near the top of the list for copiers and which offices can wait.

Denise has made her first copier selection. The company's advertising department was given top priority. Advertising needed a copier that would accept input from computer disks, do color copies, and make bound booklets for presentations. Denise selected a copier for the advertising department at a cost of $38,999. Her original budget for buying copiers contained $100,000. How much is now left in the budget for buying copiers for the other departments involved? _____

Denise next selected copiers for each of the company's nine vice presidents. To prevent any potential squabbles among them, she has chosen the same model for each vice president. It is a basic copier, capable of producing 10 color copies per minute. Each of these copiers will cost $1,250. How much money will the copiers for the vice presidents take from the overall copier budget? _____

Name _____

More About the Company Copiers

Denise is excited about the copier she has chosen for her own office. It is a compact, yet highly versatile copier. It will accept computer output, print faxes, and print in color as well. The copier also prints in laser quality, so Denise can be proud of the quality of the documents she produces. Her colleagues did not find it too surprising that Denise's office managed to make it onto the new copier priority list.

Denise's new copier cost $1,899. She also bought two extra cartridge sets at a cost of $49.99 each. Too often in the past, Denise has noticed that cartridges are often in scarce supply in the company's supply closet, and she wanted her own extra cartridge supply just for her office. Denise also purchased an on-site maintenance agreement for $225. This means that Denise can arrange maintenance for her copier just by calling a toll-free number. How much did Denise's copier cost, including the cartridges and maintenance contract? _____

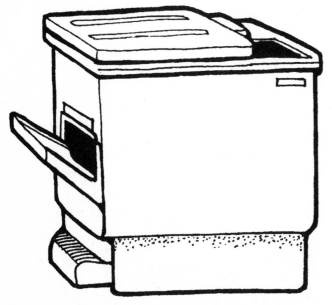

The advertising department at Denise's company won a large contract after using the copier Denise selected. The company president felt that Denise should be rewarded with a promotion for her good decision. She has been promoted to vice president of equipment and office supplies at her company. It is a brand-new position created especially with Denise in mind. The job carries a salary of $41,500 per year and has its own assigned parking space. This amount represents a whopping $16,750 more than Denise previously made. How much money was Denise making in her previous position with the company? _____

Helium Same-Day Service

Phillip owns the Cheerful Greeting Cards, Gifts, and Balloons store. He has the helium for his balloons delivered to the store in tanks from a supplier. All Phillip has to do is call the supplier by 12 noon and a new tank is delivered the same day. The supplier also picks up the empty tank at the same time.

Phillip opened the store at 9:00 a.m. and noticed that the helium tank was very low. He made a mental note to himself to call the supplier for a new tank but got busy with customers and forgot to do it. At 10:40 Phillip suddenly remembered that he had not yet called the supplier, but things were still very busy in the store. How much time does Phillip now have left to call the supplier in order to get a tank delivered that afternoon? _____

When a customer comes into the store and asks for a balloon, it takes Phillip only 4 minutes to fill the balloon with helium and ring up the customer's purchase. He has gotten really fast at doing this. Phillip has even timed himself filling the balloons, so he knows that it can be done in 4 minutes.

Phillip makes $1 profit each time a balloon is sold. How much profit would he make in 1 hour if customers came in one after another and bought balloons without stopping during the course of that hour? _____

More About Phillip and His Balloon Store

Phillip's brother, Larry, works part-time
at the Cheerful Greeting Cards, Gifts, and Balloons store.
Phillip thinks that Larry is an incompetent dunce, but family members
have pressured Phillip into hiring Larry. All of his life, Larry has messed up everything
Phillip has tried to accomplish. Once Larry left the water running and flooded Phillip's
apartment, causing him to be evicted. Another time, Larry gambled away Phillip's
Florida vacation fund on a horse race. Phillip only reluctantly hired Larry, but he plans
to watch him very closely while Larry is working in the store.

Larry seemed to be doing fine in the store, until Phillip was called away on an
emergency. When Phillip returned an hour later, the fire department had just
managed to contain the blaze. Larry had started this fire by smoking while trying to
use the helium tank. Phillip figures that his total loss from the store inventory is
$35,000. Phillip's insurance company will pay only $8,550 toward Phillip's claim, since
Larry was not listed as an employee in the company records. How much money will
Phillip lose due to Larry's negligence? _____

Phillip has begun a new balloon business
in the park. He has even invited Larry to
work for him again. Phillip is now selling
balloons from a portable cart. Whenever
the cart needs moving, he hooks it up to
Larry and makes him pull it through the
park. Phillip plans to fire Larry once he has
saved enough money to buy a horse, but
Larry will do fine until then. If Phillip has
saved $645 toward the cost of an $1,850
horse, how much more money does he
need to save before he can fire Larry and
replace him with the horse? _____

Summer Camp Chores

Ranger Bob runs a summer camp and is always encountering math problems in his work. Even during the off-season, there are always budget matters to be dealt with, bills to be paid, and supplies to be bought. Currently, Bob is checking supplies used for teaching craft classes and workshops. He wants to make certain that all the supply bins for these classes contain adequate materials for each program. For instance, Bob teaches a rope skills class to 12 students. He has noticed that the supply bin for this particular class is completely empty, having been exhausted during the last camp session. Bob will need 75 feet of rope for himself for demonstrations, and each student will need 40 feet of rope for class projects. How many feet of rope will Ranger Bob need to purchase to conduct his demonstrations and supply each student with the required amount of rope? _____

Ranger Bob has cut down a tree which was damaged by a lightning strike. He hates to waste anything, especially so much suitable wood. Normally, such a tree would just be cut into cord wood and used for campfires. Since this tree is large enough, Bob has decided instead to cut the trunk into equal pieces for his woodcarving students to use for making totem poles. The tree is 42 feet in length, but a 7-foot section is not useable due to damage from the lightning strike. There are 7 students in the carving class. How long should Ranger Bob make each piece of tree trunk? _____

More About Ranger Bob

Ranger Bob is always looking for ways to save money in his camp. He frequently reviews every aspect of camp operation to look for areas of possible savings. Bob knows that he will have 85 campers this season. He is considering a new laundry service, as the old provider kept increasing its charges. The new service has offered to pick up each camper's dirty clothes twice a week during the eight-week camp season. The laundry service requires a one-time fee of $150 to begin the service. Then it charges an ongoing rate of $3 per camper per week. The new laundry will provide a free laundry bag for each camper, so Bob thinks that the $150 up-front fee is reasonable. Including the fee to begin the new service, what will it cost Bob to use this new laundry service for the entire season? _____

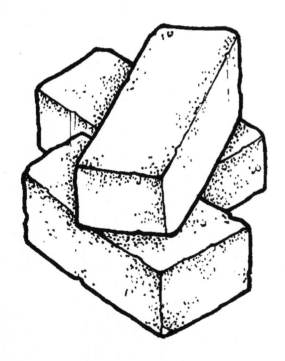

Ranger Bob has been shopping for bricks. He wants to use some of the bricks to rebuild a fireplace and the rest to help prevent soil erosion around four drainage ditches. Bob priced bricks at a local builder's supply store but found them to be too expensive for the uses he had in mind. He then checked with a supply store that carries recycled building materials and factory closeouts. Bob was able to buy 1,200 mortar bricks for $375. The bricks will be delivered to the camp free of charge.

Bob is planning to allot an equal number of bricks to each ditch but has first set aside 300 bricks for the fireplace work. How many bricks will go to each of the drainage ditches after the 300 bricks are set aside for the fireplace project? _____

Ideas Accumulate at Pet Supply

Dana is a new employee at Friendly Pet Supplies Warehouse. Friendly Pet Supplies Warehouse has a reputation for stocking a multitude of pet products. This includes food, toys, training accessories, and animal care products. Customers go there for the wide selection of pet-related products available.

Dana has noticed that nobody seems to buy the 50-pound bags of large dog biscuits, while the 5-pound bags sell quite well. She was quite surprised to count 29 of those 50-pound bags stacked on pallets. When Dana asked about the extremely large-sized bags of dog biscuits, another employee told her, "None of those 50-pound bags has ever sold since I started working here two years ago." Dana mentioned to the manager that the 50-pound bags were taking up a lot of space where better-selling products could be displayed. The manager's response was something like "our customers like to see our enormous buying power offered in a choice of product consumers cannot find with our competitors." Dana thought that it sounded like gibberish. How many pounds of dog biscuits appear to be completely unwanted by the shoppers at Friendly Pet Supplies Warehouse? _____

Friendly Pet Supplies Warehouse has a fish replacement policy for aquarium fish sold. If a fish dies within 3 days of purchase, it will be replaced with a live fish. Dana has noticed that netting and bagging a replacement fish takes an employee five minutes on average. Dana counted 48 fish replaced in one week under the fish replacement policy. How many hours of employee time were used in replacing those 48 fish during that week? _____

More About Friendly Pet Supplies Warehouse

Dana has worked very hard at Friendly Pet Supplies Warehouse. When the old store manager was fired for incompetence, Dana was the first person interviewed for the job. Her fresh ideas for returning the store to profitability found favor with the president of the company. Dana was given six months to fix the problems at the Friendly Pet Supplies Warehouse. If she can straighten things out, then the manager's job will be hers permanently.

The first thing Dana has decided to do is reevaluate each product the store carries in its inventory. Some items are dead inventory that just take up space and will never be sold. Dana's office computer shows that the store currently carries 951 different products supplied by 201 different distributors. Dana eventually decided that 67 of those products would be dropped entirely. How many different products will Friendly Pet Supplies Warehouse carry after the dropped products are removed from the shelves? _____

Dana has also decided to expand the fish business at Friendly Pet Supplies Warehouse. The old manager was not really a "fish person," but Dana sees the potential in this market. She will have an entire new wall of fish tanks set up. This will mean installing three heavy-duty shelves, each capable of holding seven fish tanks. The new shelves will cost $229 each to purchase and install. The fish tanks will cost $36 each once completely set up. How much money will the new wall of fish tanks end up costing by the time all these expenses are paid? _____

Greenhouse Soaks up the Green

Paul and his father are getting a greenhouse for their backyard. They want to give their seedlings an early start during the spring planting season. Paul and his father have been researching the subject of greenhouses and have settled on the idea of building the greenhouse themselves. Building it themselves will save a lot of money over hiring a professional contractor. The area of the country where they live does not require an expensive heating system, so this is another part of the job they will save some money on. They ordered a set of greenhouse plans for $125 that comes with a materials list, so determining what they need will be easy.

Paul and his father made a trip to a builder's supply and have purchased the materials for their greenhouse. Lumber was a big expense at $1,090. Siding and roofing materials were $869.49. Fasteners, nails, and other miscellaneous items cost $64.88. It was also discovered that they needed a special tool for cutting the siding that cost $24. If nothing else is needed during the course of building the greenhouse, what is their total cost for the greenhouse? _____

Their greenhouse plans show an interior floor space of 12 feet by 24 feet. Paul is already trying to get an idea of how much the greenhouse will hold when it is finished. He thinks that this will be adequate space to have long tables set up along each wall to hold plant trays. There might be an opportunity to hang baskets of plants or trays from the ceiling rafters as well. How many square feet of floor space will the greenhouse provide? _____

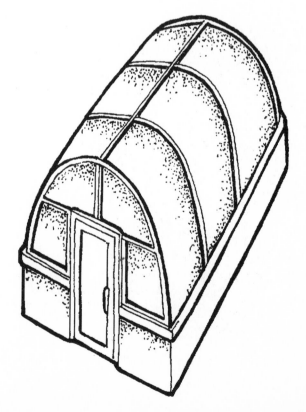

More About Paul's Greenhouse

Paul and his father were able to get the greenhouse assembled during a long weekend. Friday afternoon they worked on the project together from 1:30 p.m. until 5:00 p.m. Saturday morning they began work on the project early, beginning at 7:30. They quit work at 6:00 that evening. Sunday they completed the greenhouse, after working on it from 1:00 p.m. until 4:00 p.m. Plants still need to be brought in and seed trays begun, but that does not count toward the construction time of the greenhouse itself. How many total hours of labor were spent on the greenhouse construction project?

_____

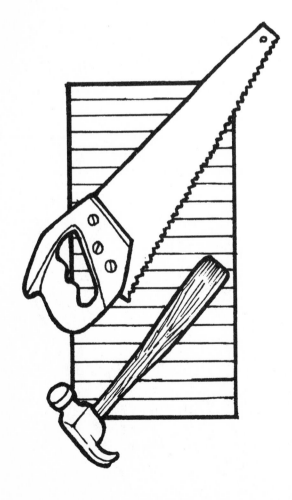

A neighbor stopped by to look at the greenhouse Paul and his father had built. The neighbor was very impressed by the quality of the job Paul had done on the greenhouse. After talking with Paul about the project, the neighbor asked if Paul would be interested in doing something similar on his property. The neighbor's greenhouse plans are a little different from the one Paul just built with his father. From looking at the plans, Paul thinks the project would take him 45 hours to complete, working by himself. The neighbor has offered Paul $900 to build the greenhouse. The neighbor will pay for all materials needed. How much will Paul make per hour if he agrees to build the greenhouse for this neighbor? _____

Community Theater Sees Success

Randy is the director of a small community theater. The theater, called The Anderson Stage, is named for the donor who purchased the building and funded the theater program.

Randy is currently producing a play. It is a modified version of a Shakespeare play, rewritten to employ more easily understood language. The production is being geared toward the school audience. Randy expects that local schools will want to book seats for field trips to the theater to see this production once opening day approaches. He plans to charge a student rate of $2 per ticket for this production and expects the theater's 425 seats to completely sell out for each performance. The play will run for only two weeks, doing ten performances in all. How much money will The Anderson Stage take in if all the performances sell out just as Randy expects? _____

Randy wants to reward each member of the theater's acting company for a good year of performances. The actors managed to regularly attract an audience to The Anderson Stage, even when the plays themselves were not particularly popular. There are 16 regular actors in the company. Randy plans to equally distribute $8,400 of surplus budget money among the regular actors. How much money will each actor receive? _____

More About the Anderson Stage

Randy has noticed that the theater's carpeting is looking stained and worn. He wants to replace the carpeting in the theater's lobby and aisles. Randy figures that the carpeting in other parts of the building can wait until next year's budget is planned and approved, but he wants this job done as soon as possible.

Randy has obtained estimates from three firms for the carpeting job. The first firm, Acme Carpets, wants $5,560 to perform the work. The second company, Ace Carpets, gave an estimate of $4,199. The third company, Trustworthy Carpets, turned in an estimate of only $2,999. But Randy has decided not to use Trustworthy Carpets, since they want their money all in cash prior to beginning any work. Randy thinks that this is a certain warning sign of fraud or shoddy work. How much money separates the estimate given by Acme Carpets from the one given by Ace Carpets? _____

Randy is planning to try a new idea. He knows that the idea is used for many sports arenas and thinks it will work for the Anderson Stage theater. Randy will set aside 40 choice balcony seats and sell those seats as season tickets. Holders of the season tickets may attend any of the performances they choose. Randy will charge $1,250 for each season ticket. How much money will the balcony season tickets generate for the Anderson Stage if all are sold? _____

115

Keen Interest in Construction

Carol has an interest in large-scale building and construction projects. She is fascinated by the notion of taking raw materials such as stone and concrete and turning them into skyscrapers, bridges, and dams.

The project she finds the most incredible by far is the Hoover Dam. Hoover Dam is situated on the Colorado River. Construction of Hoover Dam was completed in 1935. The dam itself is composed of 3,250,000 cubic yards of concrete! This exceeds even the masonry mass of the Great Pyramid of Giza. Immense loads of concrete were placed in the dam almost daily over a 24-month period. On average, how many cubic yards of concrete per month were used in constructing Hoover Dam? (State your answer to the nearest thousand.) _____

The Chesapeake Bay Bridge Tunnel spans the Chesapeake Bay connecting Norfolk and Virginia's Eastern Shore. It is a unique system of approach roads, trestles, man-made islands, and tunnels. The Bridge Tunnel was opened for traffic in 1964. In researching this project, Carol has discovered that the distance of the Bridge Tunnel's span from shore to shore is 17.6 miles. The entire structure, including the approach roads on each end, is 23 miles in length. Of the 23 total miles making up the entire structure, how many miles of the Chesapeake Bay Bridge Tunnel are approach roads? _____

Name _____

Rude Talk-Show Host Loses Ratings Battle

Hubert Stan hosts a talk show aired by radio station WDIM. The station's motto is "We may be dim, but you're listening to us." Hubert's program does not really have a theme. It is not a show about politics, sports, gardening, books, or any other specific topic. Hubert selects a few news items before each program, sometimes invites guests on, then jumps from subject to subject during the course of the show. He will try any crude gag or stunt he thinks the audience will find interesting.

One of Hubert's favorite techniques is inviting a celebrity guest to visit the show. The interview begins pleasantly enough, but Hubert gradually becomes more insulting as the interview progresses. This ambush escalates until Hubert is able to get a reaction from the celebrity. The approach may sound immature, but Hubert has brought the station's listening audience during his program to an estimated 86,000 people! Previously, the station was attracting only an estimated 33,500 listeners during this same time slot before Hubert began doing his show. What increase in listening audience has Hubert's show meant for WDIM? _____

After the newness wore off, Hubert's program began to lose its listeners rapidly. People tuning in began to think of Hubert's program as tired and unimaginative. Callers to WDIM complained that his foul language and repetitive gimmicks were boring. Hubert's program was previously heard on Monday through Friday from 3:30 p.m until 7:00 p.m. WDIM's management has decided to bring back Farmer John to do the farm report and livestock auction results from 6:00 p.m. to 7:00 p.m. Ellie the home crafter will do a call-in program, answering questions on quilting and needlepoint during the 3:30 p.m. to 4:00 p.m. time slot. How many hours per week is Hubert's program now on the air? _____

Hurricane Blows in Math Topics

Dale has been tracking the movements of a hurricane. He first heard about the hurricane only a couple of hours after it had been declared a hurricane by the weather service. Dale gets his information from watching television news reports, checking Internet sites, and by listening to a weather radio. The hurricane he is monitoring had winds of 84 miles per hour at 8 o'clock that morning. By early afternoon the hurricane's winds had increased to 95 miles per hour. That evening the strengthening hurricane was producing wind speeds of 112 miles per hour. The next morning at 8 o'clock, Dale checked the hurricane's reported wind speed. It was now 131 miles per hour. How much did the hurricane's wind speed increase during the 24 hours Dale has been monitoring it? _____

Dale has also been charting the course of this hurricane on a map. From the time the storm was first declared a hurricane, it has covered a total distance of 676 miles in 26 hours. Dale realizes that the hurricane did not travel at a constant rate of speed during this time. He has decided to figure an average speed per hour based on the time it took the hurricane to cover the distance it has traveled so far. Dale worked the figures and kept getting something that looked like a mistake. He finally realized that it was just an odd coincidence. How many miles per hour on average did this hurricane travel during the 26 hours?

_____

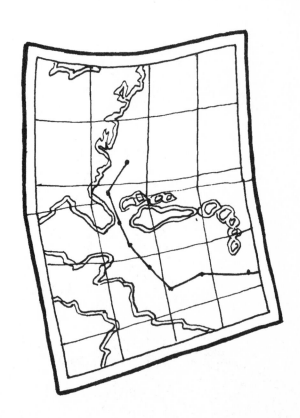

More About Dale and His Hurricane Research

The hurricane Dale was tracking finally made landfall but had weakened considerably by then. The damage it caused was far less than expected. Dale figured that the story of this hurricane was pretty much concluded and he put away the notes he had been keeping about it.

Several days later Dale was listening to a news report about the aftermath of the hurricane. Part of the story caught his attention. An insurance agent estimated that a total of $3,750,000 in damage had been done to the homes of 1,500 families living in the area hit by the hurricane. Dale pulled out his hurricane notes and jotted down the information. He realized that many of the houses mentioned by this insurance agent might have been totally destroyed, while others might have sustained only very minor damage. On average, how much damage per house was done to the homes in the area where the hurricane struck? _____

Dale was also surprised to hear about the damage done to boats along the coastline. A maritime salvage company estimated that 200 boats had either been completely lost during the hurricane or damaged beyond repair. Dale got out his hurricane notes again and did some figuring. He called a boat dealer, who told him that the average price of a new boat at the dealership was $18,000. What kind of figure will Dale enter in his hurricane notes as the total estimate for boating losses due to this hurricane? _____

Golfer Watches Score

Clayton plays most of his golf at the Hidden Creek Club. The course is well maintained and also very near his house, so it is a convenient place for him to play. Clayton also likes the lay of the course, except for two very difficult finishing holes. Clayton feels that these particular holes are exceedingly difficult, almost to the point of being unfair to the golfer.

These holes have ruined many an otherwise promising round for Clayton. They come late in the round, often catching him just a bit fatigued. Hole #16 is a long par five of 585 yards with a tight fairway. There is an annoying creek that crosses the fairway 198 yards from the tee. The creek is only 3 yards wide, but a weaker drive will roll into the creek and become unplayable. The next hole, #17, is a long par three of 187 yards. It has the smallest green on the course, sloping sharply into the woods. The hole is designed to punish those whose tee shot fails to stay on the green. If Clayton can get his drive to fall just 10 yards beyond the creek on #16, how much farther does he have to the hole? _____

Clayton is a purist when it comes to keeping his scorecard. He does not take mulligans (practice shots) or gimme putts (putts conceded by companions during stroke play). This tends to irritate some of his playing partners, but golf is the only thing in life Clayton finds he can be entirely honest about. His best score ever for a round of 18 holes was a 76, taken on a somewhat windy day when many of the holes were playing a bit short. During this particular round Clayton shot a 36 on the front nine holes. What would his score have been for the back nine holes?

_____

More About Clayton's Golfing

Clayton has fallen somewhat under the spell of corporate advertisers who tell golfers that they must have new irons, new metal woods, new putters, new bags, new shoes, or something new if they truly want to improve their game. The club pro, who coincidentally also manages the pro shop at Hidden Creek Club, has made a number of recommendations for improving Clayton's game. First, Clayton needs to buy the new titanium, gold-plated Big Bomber Oversized Driver. It costs a rather tidy $709.99 but has a larger club face than any other driver ever made. Clayton also has been told that he needs a new putter. The Zero-in alloy putter costs $239.89, but engraving of up to 22 characters is free with purchase. Clayton also has been advised to replace his irons with the new Trail Blazers, used by 14 tour professionals and modestly priced at $1,515. How much will Clayton end up spending if he follows this ridiculous advice? _____

Clayton has arranged for three clients to play golf with him at a nearby resort. (He is not taking the clients to Hidden Creek Club because he is trying to avoid the club pro there, who keeps pestering him to buy stuff!) The course where Clayton is taking his clients charges $55 per person for green fees. Clayton will be paying his own green fees and those of his clients as well. Clayton does have a discount coupon, good for $20 off a round of golf for one person. The coupon will help soften the total bill a bit. How much will Clayton spend for the golf outing? _____

Marina Manager Earns His Paycheck

Gary is the manager of Low Tide Marina. His title of manager is a bit all-inclusive since Gary is also the only employee at Low Tide Marina. His duties include leasing boat slips, handling the company books, and less glamorous chores such as taking out the office trash. Sometimes Gary puts in as many as 55 hours a week working at the marina.

The marina has 24 boat slips. (A slip is a parking space at the pier for a boat.) When all 24 slips are rented, they generate a total of $216 per day. If all the boat slips are rented for the same fee, how much does a boat slip cost at Low Tide Marina per day? _____

Gary has been forced to deal with an unusual situation. A customer brought in an old, run-down, 28-foot sailboat and rented a slip for it. The customer paid for 3 days rental in advance. After the second day, nobody recalls seeing the boat owner around the marina. But a waitress at the local diner did recall seeing the boat owner boarding a bus leaving town.

Two weeks have passed and Gary is stuck with what looks like an abandoned vessel. He has lost not only the $99 unpaid balance due on the boat slip but also has to pay a $125 fee to have the sailboat towed to the county unclaimed property yard. How much money has Gary lost altogether on this abandoned vessel?_____

Wasted Closet Space

Susan has an extra walk-in closet in her apartment. The closet has gone unused since she moved into the apartment a year ago. Susan has decided to put this extra space to good use. She has removed all the shelves and clothes hanger rods from the closet to maximize the available storage space in the closet. Susan will pack up things she does not need in cardboard boxes and stack them neatly inside the closet.

The boxes are all the same size, 2 feet on each side. She is certain that she has enough extra clothes, books, and other junk to fill up more boxes than the closet will hold. How many packed boxes will she be able to fit inside the walk-in closet if its dimensions are 8 feet deep by 6 feet wide by 7 feet tall? _____

Susan also has a spare bedroom in her apartment. She has thought of turning it into a home office, since a good bit of her work could be done at home if she had a suitable place set up for it. Susan took measurements in the room and found it to be exactly 12 feet by 14 feet. She has a pretty good idea how much office equipment would need to be moved into the room to make her home office practical. How many square feet of floor space is available in the room she is considering for an office? _____

Answer Key

Cash Register Sings at Music Store   **page 5**
Problem 1: $1,760
Problem 2: 100 times

Zoo Gets New Look   **page 6**
Problem 1: $77,500
Problem 2: $11,700

More About Barton Zoo   **page 7**
Problem 1: $3,410
Problem 2: $4,614.60

Denture Business Looks Good   **page 8**
Problem 1: $639.44
Problem 2: 538 mi

More About Ned the Denture Salesman
    page 9
Problem 1: $250
Problem 2: $1,164.11

A Transporting Hobby   **page 10**
Problem 1: $413.87
Problem 2: $2

College Budget Computed   **page 11**
Problem 1: $14,904.65
Problem 2: $70,920.00

Rainy Valley Farm Tries New Approach
    page 12
Problem 1: 179 acres
Problem 2: $17,900

More About Rainy Valley Farm   **page 13**
Problem 1: $4,125
Problem 2: $385

Modeler Meticulous About Math   **page 14**
Problem 1: 28 hours
Problem 2: $269.55

More About Conrad and His Models   **page 15**
Problem 1: $67
Problem 2: $30

Writer Keeps Up with Charges   **page 16**
Problem 1: $1,725
Problem 2: $800

Free Art Show Gets Expensive   **page 17**
Problem 1: $131
Problem 2: $400

Down at the Fish Market   **page 18**
Problem 1: $4.30
Problem 2: 240 lbs

More About the Port Harbor Fish Market
    page 19
Problem 1: $3,793.31
Problem 2: 57 lbs

Coin Collection Keeps Hobbyist Counting
    page 20
Problem 1: 2,218 pennies
Problem 2: 54 tubes

More About Danny and His Collection
    page 21
Problem 1: $3
Problem 2: $17.10

Time for a Helicopter Tour   **page 22**
Problem 1: 54 km
Problem 2: 34 min

More About Flight-Seeing Helicopter Tours
    page 23
Problem 1: $16,050
Problem 2: 248 kg

Baskets for the Making   **page 24**
Problem 1: $700
Problem 2: $270

Hikers Learn by Doing   **page 25**
Problem 1: $1,102.44
Problem 2: 48 mi

Stocks Hold Investor's Interest   **page 26**
Problem 1: $1,575
Problem 2: $870

More About Stocks   **page 27**
Problem 1: $1,200
Problem 2: $700